THE 36

BIGGEST MISTAKES
SALESMEN MAKE
AND HOW TO
CORRECT THEM

GEORGE N. KAHN

PRENTICE-HALL, INC., Englewood Cliffs, N.J.

L.C. Cat. Card No.: 63-20038

10 9 8 7 6 5 4 3 2

1st Printing   ...... March 1988 RWD CLASSICS PBK

ISBN 0-13-918961-0 PBK

ISBN 0-13-918939-4 RWD CLASSIC PBK

FOR MY WIFE, FLORENCE AND MY SON, BRUCE

Their inspiring, provocative and critical comments made this book easier to write. Since Mrs. Kahn and Bruce are officers in my company, they understood the motivating force behind me. A special thanks goes to Bruce for volunteering to act as a "guinea pig" for many of the points I raise here. As field manager for our own sales organization, he knows the pitfalls awaiting the salesman.

Mrs. Kahn knew I would be happier when I got this off my chest and she was right.

Acknowledgments

I wish to express my sincere thanks to *Sales Management* magazine for publishing the original TEN BIGGEST MISTAKES SALESMEN MAKE and for extending their permission to include the ten articles in the current volume.

I also want to thank the hundreds of sales and marketing executives around the country for their praise of the original series. Many of these men are my personal friends and supplied me with anecdotal material from their own experience and those of their men in the field.

Preface

Although hard work, imagination, and enthusiasm are essential ingredients for success in selling, a man can have all these attributes and remain a poor earner—and a single undetected mistake may be the cause. That is why I have written this book, as in my 40 years of experience in selling I have observed and noted virtually every mistake that can be made. By presenting the reader with the following 36 mistakes perhaps he will recognize his own fault, take action to eliminate it, and thereby open the way to higher earnings and progress in his profession.

Appropriately, the emphasis in this book is on correction of mistakes after they are recognized, and the mistakes I have chosen are basic ones which represent whole series of similar errors. The salesman may see in one of the 36 blunders a situation akin to the one he is experiencing. But this is just the first step. Once the fault is out in the open it must be conscientiously attacked until removed.

In the interests of keeping the salesman aware of possible inefficiencies and weaknesses in his salesmanship, this book is intended as a reference to which he can turn when problems develop. Too often the salesman is left on his own to deal with an insistent slump with only his experience and judgment to direct him and it is believed that a reading of several chapters of this book will provide a valuable aid in pinpointing the cause.

Today, as never before, the salesman must think in terms of excellence. Competition, razor-keen now, will impose even greater demands on the seller in years to come. Product differences are all but disappearing, so that what gets sold and what gathers dust in warehouses is often a matter of the salesman's competence. This trend will continue and be magnified, and the salesman can either ignore his mistakes and flounder in the frustrations of mediocrity, or he can follow the lead of today's best producers who have risen to the top through constant self-discipline applied to correcting their mistakes.

GEORGE N. KAHN

Contents

Chapter   Page

1

Rationalizing Away Sales Failures

"THE FAULT, MR. SALESMAN, IS NOT IN THE STARS BUT in yourself."

This paraphrase of advice handed out nearly 400 years ago by Shakespeare's Cassius pinpoints one of the biggest mistakes made by salesmen today: rationalizing away their own shortcomings, excusing themselves for failing to make the sale by pinning the blame somewhere else.

To illustrate: The average salesman appears before the prospect, presents his story, and hopes to come away with an order. If he succeeds, all is well—with the world and with himself. But if he fails, what happens? Chances are he will try to quickly and easily wash away his disappointment by convincing himself that:

- His product does not have all the features it should have.
- The prices he must quote are all wrong.
- The selection he can offer is too limited.
- His company's advertising campaign is no good.
- He called on the prospect at the wrong time.
- The prospect is incapable of acting in his own best interests.

- The prospect isn't really interested.
- His competitors are too far out in front.

. . Or any of a thousand all-too-familiar excuses.

Now in any given situation, of course, one or more of such rationalizations may prove to be valid reasons why he did not make the sale. But then again, they may not be valid! And this is where the trouble comes in—the salesman doesn't even bother to test the validity of the rationalization. He accepts it at face value and that is that. He automatically excuses himself from any personal responsibilities for having let that sale slip away.

At no point does this salesman sit down and honestly ask himself where he personally may have been at fault. Did he, for example, fail to gain the prospect's full attention at the start of the interview? Did he fail to satisfactorily answer one or more objections the prospect raised? Did he wait too long before attempting to "close"? Did he place too little emphasis on product quality . . . fail to emphasize service features . . . have an inadequate grasp of the prospect's business and problems?

Important questions, yes! But hard questions for a salesman to ask, because they demand a good deal of soul searching.

And because they are hard questions to face, the salesman simply doesn't bother to ask them. He takes the easy way out, instead, and reverts to those oh-so-ready rationalizations. Thus he may blame various departments within his own company for failing to give him the right sort of product or selling support. He may blame his competition for getting to the prospect first, for using unfair sales arguments, for making special concessions. He may even blame the unsold prospect, by reassuring himself that ". . . no one could get through to that guy!" And who knows but what there are salesmen who even go so far as to blame the stars! Happily, because all such factors clearly lie outside himself, the salesman is delivered from the task of self-examination or self-criticism.

This continued ego-soothing manages to bury selling mistakes even deeper. They become even more firmly embedded into the salesman's day-to-day approach. Experience for such a man is not a teacher. It is, instead, a conditioner that reinforces and magnifies his past mistakes. He moves on a one-way street that inevitably leads to successive selling failures.

But there is no law that says a salesman must remain on such a sales-defeating street. Many a man has been able to detour suddenly onto the road that leads to selling success. All it takes are three things: the willingness to face up to the fact that selling failures are generally attributable to the salesman himself; the courage to dig out these buried mistakes; and the ambition to seek the wisdom and skills to avoid making them in the future.

To accomplish this important transition from rationalization to reason (and it can be done at any stage in a salesman's career), one should have an organized approach. This is not a matter of making good resolutions today and sliding back into rationalizations next week. It requires self-discipline and continuing efforts. The salesman must look at himself in the mirror, so to speak, time after time after time—and learn from what he sees.

Sales managers can suggest these three steps to salesmen who are trying to break out of the rationalization rut:

1. Analyze Each Selling Failure

"Why did I *really* lose the sale? Where did I go wrong? At what point—or points—and why, did I lose the prospect? Did he seem to be annoyed by my personal mannerisms? Did I have sufficient information on his company, his needs, etc.? Where did I bog down in handling his objections? Did I cover all product features?"

These are but a few of the many questions a salesman might seriously ask himself after failing to make a sale. And with experience, of course, he will eventually be able to narrow such questions down to those which have most meaning in terms of his own sales approach and/or the nature of a given sales situation.

It is almost as though he were a newspaper reporter covering a given event. He must ask every question that might possibly lend clarity to his report of what happened and why.

Then the salesman must carefully analyze his own report, seeking out and admitting the mistakes that show up. And he must, of course, take measures to see that these mistakes do not recur in the future. If, for example, he finds that on a number of occasions he did not have sufficient information about prospects' requirements, he will make a point of briefing himself more fully before all future calls. If he finds there's a particular customer objection that inevitably leaves him stumbling over his words, he'll make sure to develop a satisfactory reply.

Occasionally, a salesman should also turn his questions upon a sales situation that went well—where he actually came away with a good order. By determining what he "did right" in such situations, he will often be able to spot where he has gone wrong in less successful presentations.

2. Discuss Failures with Other Salesmen

A cousin of mine, a surgeon, recently told me of an interesting group to which he belongs. It is composed of ten men, all surgeons. Whenever one of these men believes an operation might have gone more successfully, he asks the other members to meet with him in a problem seminar. Here he will discuss the operation, the reasons for his dissatisfaction, where he thinks he might have proceeded differently, and so forth. The members then offer comments, based upon their analyses of the information presented and their own experiences.

Certainly this technique applies to any profession. A salesman is extremely well advised, in short, to discuss his problems with other salesmen. This affords him an element of objectivity that might be lacking in his self-questioning and analysis. And it allows him to profit from the steps that other salesmen have taken to successfully overcome similar problems.

While it is most likely that a salesman will choose to discuss his selling failures with other salesmen from his company, there is just as much likelihood he can profit from discussions with salesmen from other firms. Indeed, he may profit even more, since he may feel more relaxed about "confessing" his shortcomings to those with whom he is not, in effect, competing. And they, in turn, may be freer and more objective in offering suggestions and revealing their own sales problems.

The important thing, however, is that the discussions take place. Too often the salesman, like the fisherman, only talks of his work when he's landed a big one. Today's salesman must also be willing to talk of the ones that shouldn't have got away, *but did.* Seriously entered, such group discussions can be among the most educational experiences available.

3. Check with the Boss

Many a sales manager has complained to me that his biggest training problem is not knowing exactly where his salesmen are having troubles. As one such manager told me, "How can I help these guys when they'll never admit where they need help?"

Well, how can he? Yet even salesmen who've gotten over the habit of hiding mistakes from themselves will often prefer to make no mention of these mistakes to their boss. What a wealth of possible insights and ideas these men are denying themselves. The very fact that the boss is the boss is testimony that he's probably overcome similar selling problems in the past (you can bet he has long since learned to replace rationalization with reason). And I have yet to meet the sales manager who isn't ready, willing, and anxious to pass down the experience and know-how he's gained over the years.

Obviously, many salesmen hesitate to discuss their selling mistakes with the boss because they fear this will put them in an unfavorable light. But they should be made to realize that if they haven't been turning in sales they are probably already in an unfavorable light. And that, in any event, if they are subsequently able to eliminate such mistakes and increase their sales they are bound to look better.

Incidentally, I have yet to meet the sales manager who didn't look up to the salesman who came to him and said, in effect, "Look, I'm having a problem. I think I am doing such and such wrong. Do you agree, and if so what corrective measures should I take?" This is the mark of a man who's really in there pitching and, even more important, a man who is *thinking*. Every salesman should understand that this is what sales managers are looking for today in building their organizations, granting increases, and picking their possible successors.

2

Coming Back with the Same Old Pitch

A PURCHASING AGENT BY THE NAME OF DAVE CURRY recently told me this story: One salesman called on Dave time and time again without getting an order. Finally, he broke down and complained, "You know, Mr. Curry, no matter how many times I come back here I always get the same story." Dave replied: "Well, look at it from my point of view. One of the main reasons you haven't gotten an order is that every time you've come here you've told me the same old story."

Dave's reply is a classic because it so well illustrates one of the major shortcomings of most salesmen today. They simply fail to vary their sales presentation when they face a prospect they have called on before.

Sales prospects don't relish the idea of being bored to tears by the same old sales pitch rendered in the same old way by the same salesman who looks the same old way and uses the same old arguments.

Yet that's exactly what happens day after day. Just ask any

group of executives who are charged with buying responsibility. And it's one of the reasons that so many repeat sales calls fail to pay off as they should. Matter of fact, it is probably also the reason why so many salesmen find it harder and harder to get back into the buyer's office at all.

This is a tough point to hammer home to salesmen. They generally buy the concept readily enough, but often balk at the implementation. "What do you want me to do?" they ask. "Stand on my head while I deliver my sales talk? Paint my product a different color? Wear bells?"

What is really wanted is for them to enjoy the sort of sales call they're always hoping for—the type that results in sales. And to accomplish this, a salesman must take himself out of the common variety of "callers" most buyers dismiss routinely.

If standing on one's head or wearing bells would help bring this about, they might merit a degree of consideration. But no such radical approach is generally needed. What is needed is a sharper realization that prospects want to see, hear, and learn something different each time the salesman calls. Only under such conditions will they be likely to grant him the audience he wishes. Only under such conditions will they give him the time and attention he needs to really sell his product and come away with an order.

What can a salesman do to bring such conditions about? Primarily, he must recognize the factors that underlie a buyer's willingness to grant an audience in the first place. He must know why the prospect is willing to listen.

There are three such basic motivations. Each is vitally important, though one may be present to a much greater degree than the others in any given sales situation. Before he calls, every salesman should do his best to determine why he is being welcomed again, and should be prepared to satisfy this unspoken condition of entry.

The three big reasons why salesmen are allowed to make repeat calls are:

1. Because the customer or prospect hopes to learn something new about the product.
2. Because he hopes to learn something new about his business or industry.
3. Because he simply expects to enjoy the meeting.

. . . Something New About the Product

Few persons like to sit through the same movie a second time. Even fewer would be willing to do so a third or fourth time. Yet this is exactly what many salesmen seem to expect of their prospects. They come into the office with the same presentation, run through it in the same manner, stress the same points—all without changing a word.

No wonder the prospect is half asleep before the salesman is half way through his presentation, if, indeed, he allows it to continue to the end! And no wonder the odds are so great that the prospect will again turn thumbs down on the request for an order.

For the prospective buyer to actually give an order, would, in fact, place him in the position of reversing the negative or neutral decision he made at the conclusion of the previous sales call. No one, after all, likes to do that. It goes against sound psychology.

In order for this prospect to change his decision now, he has to be given brand-new "reasons why."

What sort of reasons? Obvious ones are product changes and improvements, new service features offered by the manufacturer, new price factors, etc. Obvious, yes. But it is surprising—indeed, amazing—how often salesmen will underplay these factors (perhaps with the exception of price reductions) in repeat presentations.

There's always the possibility, of course, that there have been no such basic changes since the salesman's last call. In this case it becomes all the more important for the salesman to alter

his presentation so that the old appears new. "Perhaps I men·
tioned this before," he might say, "but I don't believe I clearlv
explained the many advantages involved. Otherwise I'm cer·
tain you'd have ordered it on the spot." Or he might even emphasize why certain features of his product have not been
changed—because they provide an unmatched level of performance, etc.

Examples are unlimited in number, but the point remains
the same: on a repeat call, every sales story must have an element of news that provides the prospect with a new set of
reasons why he should buy.

Such change and re-emphasis is particularly important, of
course, where the salesman uses a basically canned presentation.
Believe it or not, some salesmen will call back time after time
with the same speech, word for word. Such canned materials,
at best, serve only as mental outlines. It is up to the salesman
to alter and adapt, keeping them from becoming mental ruts.

. . . Something New About the Industry

One of the most successful salesmen I know is a gold mine
of information on executive changes in the industry to which
he sells. Everyone, he says, likes to know who's going where and
why in competitive organizations—and he always tries to have
the latest information on the tip of his tongue. This makes
prospects willing, even eager, to talk with him, and paves the
way for his sales presentation.

Possibilities for this type of approach are many. The important thing is for the salesman to make sure his information
is as complete as possible, and not yet too well known in the
field.

This need not involve the salesman in any form of under-
cover work. A surprising amount of data can be gathered from
daily newspapers, trade association reports and contacts, trade

publications, etc. Surprisingly, few salesmen seem to avail themselves of this information and/or put it to work.

Somewhat related is the approach of the salesman who manages to provide new insights and ideas that can help the prospect improve his own business. One salesman I know always brings the prospect a suggestion for solving a problem discussed during his previous visit. Of course, this requires a good deal of homework on the salesman's part; he's even been known to contact outside business specialists in arriving at a solution. But it places him on a special pedestal in the minds of his customers. He's more than a salesman; he's a business confidant and advisor. And he gets more orders than any other salesman in his field.

. . . Making the Meeting Enjoyable

Take ten salesmen of comparable backgrounds and skills; give each a similar product; and have them call on the same customer. How many will be welcomed back a second time? How many a third? How many a fourth? Any experienced sales manager knows that the number will decrease at each successive stage of the call-back procedure. Perhaps five of the ten salesmen will be afforded a satisfactory hearing the third time around, but it's highly doubtful that more than one or two will be as welcome on the eighth, ninth, or tenth call as on the first one.

Why this difference? Why is one salesman given the key to the buyer's office, while another has a difficult time obtaining even a second hearing? The answer is to be found in the fact that some salesmen—unfortunately too few—are able to provide the customer or client with what can best be described as a "psychological lift." These are the salesmen who—quite apart from the presentation of their products or their ideas—continually manage to provide a personal sense of the new and the unexpected.

One of the most effective "lifters" of buyer interest I've ever known is my good friend Sam Cornell—a master salesman if there ever was one. For a long while Sam's favorite gimmick was to enter a buyer's office carrying a bag of what he liked to call "sales refreshments." One time it would be a bag of hot chestnuts, another time a bag of marshmallows, or dried prunes or pretzel sticks. After a while Sam's bag got to be pretty much the talk of the industry, and many a buyer—and his secretary— could hardly wait till Sam came around so they could confirm their guesses as to what that bag would hold.

A trifle bold perhaps? Maybe it would seem so to the average salesman who assumes that anything so different might subject him to ridicule. But then, Sam was no average salesman—nor was his income average.

Not all salesmen will wish to go so far as Sam, of course. But that doesn't mean they can't do something to make their sales visits more noteworthy in the buyer's mind. I know one sales- man, for example, who has never worn the same tie while call- ing on the same buyer. He carries a wide selection of neckwear in his car, and by consulting a little record book he's able to make the appropriate change before calling on the next cus- tomer.

"A few of my customers," he says, "never really notice the difference. But most do—and it has become a matter of con- siderable interest to them. Guessing what sort of tie I'll be wearing seems to bring a little extra fun into their daily rou- tine. And it always gets our meeting off to an informal and relaxed start."

Both of these examples are, of course, obvious, physical things. In other cases it could be that the salesman is such an interesting person buyers will look forward to seeing him.

But it's not the nature of the "gimmick" that counts so much as the idea: the salesman can no more allow uniformity to creep into his manner and appearance than the company he represents can allow dullness and lack of innovation to creep into its products.

The average buyer today has a far more difficult job than most salesmen seem willing to realize. He sees not one but many salesmen each day, and he may in the course of a year see the same man time and time again. The great majority of these salesmen will prove dull beyond belief—dull in manner, dull in appearance, dull in the presentation of the product.

The salesman who makes an effort to bring new life into each of these areas is the one who will be rewarded. He will get the time and attention he desires, and he'll greatly increase his chances of getting the sale.

3

Giving Up Too Quickly

A YOUNG MAN NAMED HARRY WAS EMPLOYED AS AN assistant manager by a client of mine. Passing his desk one day I noticed a photo of an attractive girl.

"Is that your wife?" I asked.

He shook his head wistfully. "No, I'm afraid she doesn't give me much of a tumble. I dated her two or three times, but afterwards when I tried to continue our relationship it was no dice. First she had a headache and the next time she said she was busy."

"And what about the times after that?"

"That was it," Harry said. "I don't like to make a pest of myself. Besides, I can tell when I'm getting the brush-off."

It took some fast talking to get him to change his mind. "Maybe she did have a headache, and she probably was busy. Those things do happen to people," I reasoned.

The point reached home, and Harry's consequent success in pursuing his case—and his quarry—was not surprising.

It's probably not an exaggeration, however, to say that there are far more salesmen who give up too easily than there are reluctant Romeos. Men who would chase a woman to the ends of the earth often fail to persevere in a simple selling situation.

Many salesmen have become qualified experts in rationalizing themselves out of persistency. Every sales manager has heard his men say that Saturday is a bad time to call, or that you can't call on a prospect before lunch, or on Friday afternoon, or before he has had time to read his mail, or if it is a rainy day.

One of the biggest mistakes a salesman can make is to conjure up a bunch of bogey men and permit them to stand in the way of pushing home his selling points as often—and as persuasively—as possible.

The 20 Percent That Keep Trying

Studies show that 48 percent—almost half—of all salesmen quit cold after a single call on a prospect. Another 20 percent make two calls before quitting; 7 percent make three, and 5 percent make four calls.

The remaining 20 percent make five calls or more, and these are the men who get from 75 percent to 80 percent of the business.

These are the men who persevere—and without perseverance there can be no success. This is true in every walk of life, but it is especially true in selling.

I know a golf pro, a tournament player, who practices until he has blisters on his hands. In a way this man's raw flesh is a symbol of his perseverance. His reward is a national reputation, fame and fortune.

Throughout history there are innumerable examples—from Joan of Arc to Commander Alan Shepard—to prove that the great things in life were attained only by the tremendous sacrifices of outstanding human beings. In a relatively short span of years we have progressed from the laboriously slow oxcart to our present era of jet-propelled flight, with more dramatic progress still to come.

Without the beyond-the-call-of-duty efforts and sacrifices

made by certain engineers, businessmen and people of science, we would still be crawling through life instead of flying.

Management would do well to keep that 48 percent record of quitters in mind. It would be a giant step in the direction of success if they could remember it—and understand why almost half of all salesmen make just one call and give up. Despite the superhuman effort sometimes demanded of them, salesmen are human. And being human, they tend to take the easy way out.

As all sales managers know, a natural barrier is often set up between the prospect and the salesman. This is part of the selling game. Purchasing agents, executives and businessmen in general are a busy lot. In order to stave off the many individuals who are constantly making demands on their time, they develop what may seem to be a hostile attitude. They may appear curt, brusque, unapproachable. This is nothing more than an act, a device designed to conserve precious time by getting rid of the easy quitters as quickly as possible.

But men who buy, in spite of their ogre-like histrionics, are really no different from men who sell. They have their problems and mishaps, individual triumphs and failures, and, in a sense, their own quotas to fulfill.

Once a salesman recognizes this and refuses to be rebuffed by the artificial barrier, his chance of doubling and tripling his income will skyrocket. The man who calls on his prospect, and keeps on calling and calling and calling, is the man who will come out on top. The big mistake most of the quitters make is forgetting that the customer, too, is a human being.

There Is Always a Reason

A salesman can't call back too often as long as he has something to say, something new and interesting to impart to the prospect. One top salesman adheres to this creed religiously: "Never call back on a prospect just to ask for an order. If you have nothing to say, don't call back. If you do have something to say—an interesting, useful and informative message to relay—call back a hundred times."

And, of course, if a salesman has nothing to say it is a short-coming on his part. If he looks hard enough he can always find something to say. He can learn more about his product and how it can help his prospects. He can bone up on his prospect's business, learn what its problems are and how he can help solve them. The extra effort will give him a friend for life, a friend who will always be glad to see him.

Granted, the glad welcome is always more pleasant and heart-warming than the cold rebuff. But cold rebuffs are as much a part of the selling game as the sample case. They should be regarded as walls in need of storming. I think that giving in to discouragement is nothing more than taking the easy way out. In this business of selling, discouragement and failure go hand in hand. Discouragement is a luxury no salesman can afford.

The surest way to slay the dragon of discouragement is by expending an extra bit of effort. In selling language, that means calling back again and again and again and then, when you feel you have just about had it, make one more call.

This is the call that really counts the most. And this is the call that every sales manager must demand of his men.

4

Being a Two-Dimensional Man

IT'S NO TRICK TO RECOGNIZE MOST MISTAKES MADE BY salesmen.

A perceptive supervisor can spot many errors immediately. Or the man himself may spot his own faults and iron them out with time. The man who is, say, sloppy in appearance or coarse-mannered has an obvious failing. And the remedy, too, is pretty obvious.

But there is another kind of mistake, a very big one that you won't find covered in the usual guide books for salesmen. It flashes no warning signal, yet its detection is vital to the sales-man's success and well-being.

This is the mistake of being a "lopsided" man, a two-dimensional individual who never develops his true potential for living. Such a man equates existing with living and never realizes the difference. He is not a whole man. His two activities are working and sustaining life. As a person, he is fast beating a path to mediocrity.

You have seen this man. He has never achieved a proper balance among work, play, love, and spiritual values. He has never gotten beyond his own narrow enclosure, even to the extent of tasting a new dish. A suggestion that he develop an avocation draws only a blank stare. He is a fractional man.

What does all this have to do with selling?

Plenty.

A successful salesman must work hard, but if he single-mindedly excludes all other activities, he fails. He fails himself, his family, his employer, and his customer. A drudge will be treated for what he is by his clients. A "whole man" emits a spark, a zest for living lacking in the dull plodder. The lopsided salesman may get his order from time to time, but his prospects are as limited as his horizon.

The Third Dimension

The well-balanced man, on the other hand, is sought out by friends and customers alike. He possesses a magnetism that attracts business, often without any apparent effort on his part.

Selling, after all, depends on the personal contact. Mere information can be written into an advertisement; personality, humanity, the enjoyment of knowing and liking cannot. This is a basic reason why the good salesman can never be replaced by the printed word—and why the two-dimensional man offers little more than you can get from paper and ink.

Let me tell you the story of a good friend, Lou Clark who rose from humble beginnings to become one of the most successful and prosperous service salesmen in this country.

It is not a conventional rags-to-riches yarn.

After he was graduated from high school, Lou drifted from job to job. One day, just after World War I, he heard about a competitive examination for the position of supercargo in the Merchant Marine.

He took the exam and rated high. In the years that followed he traveled to most of the world's ports. He spent the long months at sea filling the gaps in his knowledge by reading voraciously. His books became the college he hadn't been able to afford.

He also acquired a love of travel which never left him.

After his separation from the Merchant Marine, Lou went into one of the service businesses. He began the hard way by cold canvassing New York, and in a very short time became one of the top men in his field.

His success was not accidental. Much of what he gained came as a result of his seafaring days. Lou was not the type of traveler who gains only surface impressions of a foreign country. In addition to taking hundreds of interesting pictures abroad, he talked to scores of natives and officials in an effort to really know and understand the people.

When he began his business career he occasionally invited his friends to an informal showing of his slides. Not only were the illustrations fascinating, but his lectures were so interesting that more and more friends and acquaintances wanted to hear him.

As his business improved, Lou resumed globe-trotting on his holidays. At first he took off from three to six weeks a year. In later years, his business success assured, he journeyed abroad for as long as six or seven months at a stretch.

Lou was not a mere performer. He became a well-rounded man whose avocation opened doors forever closed to the lopsided individual. Friends and customers sought him out. What began as small social gatherings for slide lectures eventually turned into a big business in itself. Commercial movie travelogues produced by Lou were shown around the world.

Success was piled on success. He was publicized by major magazines; his reputation put him in contact with high government officials; a nationally known explorers' organization elected him president. During World War II, the government commissioned him for important assignments overseas.

Success came to Lou Clark because he never stopped growing. Of course, he worked hard in his service business, but he was not satisfied with that treadmill existence. He made himself interesting and informative through his avocation.

Now, most salesmen can't trek off to the African wilds to round out their personalities. Obviously, Lou's life style cannot be copied by everyone.

But anyone can—and should—build an outside interest or activity to give his life a sense of balance. The rewards may not be immediate, but in the long run this balance will become a sort of negotiable currency. The exchange commodity? Achievement, simple happiness, success in its broadest meaning.

More Than Putting in Time

Material gain is bound to follow. By presenting to customers and business associates the personality of a whole man, the well-rounded salesman has a selling factor which the lopsided man can never possess. Even in these hard-fact days of "unemotional" buying, business will gravitate towards the man who has something extra to offer.

The mistake of being a lopsided man can be corrected. The salesman must look beyond himself. He must try to imagine how he appears to others. He must ask himself, "Am I just putting in time in life?" If the answer is "yes," he must do something about it. The road to a richer life is open. He who takes it will be a better salesman—and a better man.

5

Spurning Available Facts and Figures

HARRIS JUST WASN'T PRODUCING ON HIS NEW JOB. He had been a top man for a competitor, and had been lured away because of his outstanding performance. Then he fizzled.

Now, a topnotch man doesn't suddenly become a third-rater without cause; there is generally a good reason, and Harris' case was no exception.

The obvious possibilities—health, family, money, etc.—could be ruled out quickly. This time the cause was a little more deeply hidden.

The answer was discovered soon enough. In his old job, Harris had relied heavily on certain selling tools provided by the home office: statistics, sales analysis reports, market analyses, and so on. He was in a tough, competitive business and he got everything out of these aids that he could.

In his new job, however, he was trying to go it alone.

The tools Harris received from his new boss were every bit as effective as those he had used on his old job. But two factors had changed. On the old job, he was closely supervised. His management made sure the selling tools were used properly.

In his new position he was more on his own. Secondly, report formats vary from company to company, and Harris just hadn't bothered to learn the new system.

Harris was an "anti-paperwork" salesman by nature. Any activity which interrupted his regular calls he considered a waste of time. On the old job he derived an advantage from the company's information flow because he had no other choice but to use it. Without thinking, he took his sales tool box for granted.

Now he suddenly found reports and statistics difficult to understand because they were new and different. So, instead of taking the time and patience to understand the data furnished him, he set it aside and almost ruined his career.

Be Armed—Or Be Vulnerable

Salesmen fail to realize that times and methods are changing drastically. Today's sales picture and that of fifteen years ago are as different as a Rembrandt is from a Matisse. Each year business becomes more specialized, more competitive.

A new factor has been added: science. To ignore or resist it is about as sound as making sales calls in a horse and buggy. Yet countless salesmen who should know better are still trying to operate without it (and the selling help it offers).

Today the successful salesman must venture forth into battle armed with facts. When salesmen lack such ammunition they are vulnerable—and the competition will be sure to find these chinks in the sales armor.

This is where the home office comes in. Today's sales and marketing technology is taking the guess-work out of selling. Computers, punch card equipment and advanced marketing techniques are accurately forecasting sales potential by area, consumer class, economic level and whatnot. Industrial trends are being taken into consideration, and figures showing rate and extent of proposed new product penetration, performance of competitive products and so on are developed as a matter of course.

One ball-of-fire salesman told me: "Statistics! Couldn't oper·ate without them. They tell me where to call and when. They alert me to specific needs of my established accounts. They are the tools I urgently need to develop new business. Without statistics I'd feel like a naked kid trying to buck a regiment of armored tanks."

I recently spoke with the sales director of a major equipment manufacturer who had worked up to his present job via the field sales route. He frowned when he said: "Getting people to use facts and figures is one of my biggest headaches. I keep trying to impress my men with the importance of paperwork in sales and in all aspects of the business. Some of them are opposed to paperwork by nature; others are beginning to see the light. The results speak for themselves. The top men are the ones who put the information flow to use. If I hadn't believed this I would not be holding the job I enjoy today."

You can take almost any product today and there will be another just like it to do the job as well, if not better. The honeymoon is over, and has been for some time now. The wartime and boomtime insatiable demand for virtually any and all products is a thing of the past.

Today, if a prospect is to favor you with the business instead of the next guy, you have to come up with quality and service. You, your salesmen, and your company must consistently produce impressive and worthwhile innovations. Without fast, accurate and effective two-way communications this is a difficult, if not impossible, feat to accomplish. Ideas are needed, and facts —from both ends of the line.

If a company pours forth information to the salesman, as all progressive firms are doing today, and the salesman relegates this material to the trunk compartment of his car or the drawer of his desk, it is as if management had made an expensive long distance call to a wrong number.

A Look in the Trunk

A salesman I know, named Al, used to spend ten hours a week going through invoice copies to determine what was bought by each of his accounts. He worked long rows of figures on big sheets and went through some mathematical acrobatics for which he was ill equipped. Finally he evolved information concerning activity, stock shortages and the like, which he deemed vital to his selling job.

Tapping the thick sheaf of papers proudly, he said: "This is my brain. Without this baby, I wouldn't know where I am."

"Al," I said quietly, "let's see the reports you get from the home office."

He produced a stack of reports from the trunk of his car. Then I sat down with him and showed how the figures he had spent ten hours to develop were all duplicated on the reports he had never bothered to work with. He could have come up with the same guidance material in thirty minutes instead of ten hours.

Part of Al's problem was that he was a top salesman. Like so many other producers, he figured that no one could tell him anything. You can't argue with success—but no salesman's success is ever really quite complete.

Al's "success" was reflected by a $13,000 income. He spent a fourth of his working week duplicating information that was available in a half hour. On this basis, his income should have been more than $16,000 instead of $13,000.

Here's another example: There was a crack salesman named Joe Burns who worked for one of our client companies. After almost every calendar period, or at the close of virtually every sales contest, Joe was sure to emerge on top. But Joe was not a typical sales leader: He had gotten into sales late, after spending the early part of his career in the accounting department.

This background was responsible for much of his success.

Over the years he had watched with great interest as much vitally needed statistical information was presented to the salesmen in weekly, monthly, and quarterly doses. Sometimes he sat in at sales meetings. Eventually, he arrived at a rather interesting conclusion:

"These fellows aren't using half the information given them. They go into the field so poorly equipped to do the job it's a wonder they make out at all. Now, this is a good, successful company. Our salesmen are as good as any in the industry. It must be, then, that our competitors' salesmen are going into the field as poorly equipped as ours are—or else they'd be killing us.

"Heck, any guy with sense enough to use this statistical information to the hilt could make a real killing."

From that day on, Joe tried to get into sales. When he finally did, his top-flight performance paid more eloquent tribute to his reasoning than any words could do.

In the years ahead, facts and figures will become increasingly vital to the sales function as competition from abroad becomes more and more fierce.

The business equipment industry, with giants like IBM, RCA, NCR and Remington Rand leading the way, have accepted this challenge with admirable gusto. Today's computers digest and process business facts at speeds of microseconds (millionths of a second). They are coming up with more significant and more reliable information than ever before, and in time to be useful in bringing home sales and determining product needs.

Can a salesman duplicate this effort with a pencil and paper? Or can he afford to ignore it entirely?

The answer is pretty obvious. Now only the salesmen must be convinced.

6

Ignoring the Customer's Customer

WHEN GENERAL FOODS ADVERTISES IN A NATIONAL MAGA-
zine . . . or Procter & Gamble launches a spot TV campaign,
they are concerned not so much with selling their supermarket
customers as with creating demand and profit by selling their
customers' customers.

That this kind of approach brings results needs no testimony.
But, for some reason, the typical salesman—and sales manager—
seems to feel that this technique is owned and copyrighted by
the advertising department.

It isn't though—and the mere fact that "second-generation"
marketing is ignored on the sales line is one of the biggest
mistakes in selling today.

Jack Irwin, one of the most successful sales managers I know,
doesn't let his salesmen make this mistake. Instead, he consistently racks up sales records for his industry, simply by
requiring his salesmen to make at least one call on a customer's
customer for every ten they make on the customers themselves.
In this case the salesmen, whose job is to sell fabrics to the
manufacturers of women's wear, find themselves calling on
most of the major department stores and specialty shops.

The purpose of such calls, Jack emphasizes, has nothing to do with making a sale. That's clearly the job of the garment manufacturer's own sales force. Jack's salesmen, by contrast, are engaged in what he describes as a combined market research and sales promotion function.

The salesman will ask, for example, how a given line or model of coat is moving, and why the answer happens to be "fast," "slow," or "just average." If the retailer seems to be dissatisfied, the salesman will seek out suggestions for ways in which the cut or style of the garment might be improved. "And, quite naturally," Jack points out, "he'll show how our fabrics have been used and give the retailer pointers on how the quality of such fabrics can be translated into positive selling points."

Retailer Turns Salesman

The retailer's reaction to such calls is uniformly favorable. He's surprised and delighted that his "supplier's supplier" will make this extra effort. And he's grateful for the merchandising and selling tips he picks up.

"You can be sure," says Jack Irwin, "that the retailer will mention our man's call to his supplier—our customer—and in a most positive way. And many has been the time that a retailer has asked other manufacturers why they, too, don't use our fabrics. So, in effect, this retailer becomes a salesman for our product, and a darned good one, too."

One more dividend results from these calls on customers' customers. Since the retailer will sometimes be more frank and objective with one of Jack's men than he will be with his supplier's own salesmen, information gathered in such calls can be profitably played back to the manufacturer. Jack Irwin, in short, is able to provide his own customers with what amounts to a hip-pocket market research service. This pays off, he says, in closer ties with his customers, and provides a bit of extra value which helps keep competitors out of his markets.

The fabric business is by no means the only one which can profit by this indirect selling technique. It really doesn't matter what you sell, even if your product becomes completely un-identifiable by the time it reaches your customer's customer. This same call approach has been utilized successfully by tele-vision tube manufacturers, chemical companies and steel com-panies, to name but a few. You name the industry, and chances are it can sell via the customer's customer.

Second-generation advertising is terrifically successful, but imagine how much more effective contacts with the customer's customer can be when carried out personally by a firm's own salesmen. A salesman not only carries the message down the line but also brings a message back. The total effect is magni-fied and the sales force has all the more ammunition with which to fire away.

Even if these third-party calls served no other purpose, they would more than justify themselves in the training they give a salesman. The salesman who is able to talk intelligently from firsthand experience about his customer's selling prob-lems is going to have one whale of an advantage. He's going to be better able to deal with that customer, and he's going to be able to help his own company do a better job of tailoring its products to the customer's needs.

Occasionally an Order

Although the third-party call is mainly an informational or a good will device, occasionally an order will develop out of such a call. The salesman who is so blessed is in an unbeatable posi-tion to further cement his relationship with his grateful cus-tomer.

In addition, there are times when obtaining orders from the

customer's customer becomes a salesman's primary goal. For example:

A year or so ago we were approached by the manager of a company that had come up with a really superior ball point pen. But there were already so many ball point pens on the market that the company couldn't get any major office supply firms to stock it. Their salesmen called and called again, but to no avail.

Within six months, however, this company's pen was the eighth best seller in this gigantic field—a field dominated by literally scores of firms who have been long established and respected.

How was it done? By sending the company's sales staff out to call on business offices in major buildings instead of on office supply firms. They'd take a building and visit floor after floor, talking with every office manager they could possibly see. By the end of each day they would have a stack of orders for a trial quantity of their pens. By the end of the week this stack of orders had grown tall indeed. Then it was time to call on the office supply houses once again. This time they didn't go begging for orders. They went in with orders right in their hands— orders from customers these dealers would like to be selling.

"How would you like to fill these orders?" they would ask the dealer. Stock the line in the future? Of course, they'd just *love* to. In a matter of days the manufacturer had his product on every shelf it could have desired.

What this amounted to, of course, was nothing less than pulling merchandise through the channels of distribution. It is a form of selling that is just getting under way in many fields today. With the need so great, and the results so marked, it promises to be a technique that all of us in marketing are going to be hearing a lot more about. And it represents only one variation—albeit an important one—on the technique of selling the customer's customer.

If any moral need be drawn, perhaps it could be this: No

salesman today can afford to neglect the opportunity of making personal calls on the customer's customer. It is no task to discover who these third parties are. It requires no great effort or time outlay to visit them—showing how your product adds of the value of the product they normally purchase, asking their suggestions for product improvements, passing on suggestions for better merchandising and selling, and so on.

As sales manager Jack Irwin might add: For a salesman to devote one out of every eleven calls to his customer's customer is to multiply the chances that the other ten calls will pay off big in sales.

7

Flouting the Law of Attrition

THE SALESMAN'S JOB IS TO SELL, NOT TO MEMORIZE A LOT of economic theory. Yet, there is one "law" of economics which bears directly on his income and which he should know cold: the "law" of customer attrition.

It is simply this: The same customers do not stay on a salesman's books year after year after year. There is an inevitable dropping off or attrition that is currently running at an average company rate of from 3.5 percent to 6 percent a year. The individual salesman, however, may lose no accounts—or all his accounts—to attrition in any given year.

What every salesman should burn into his mind, therefore, is that this attrition will happen whether he is the top producer or the rock-bottom man, and it will happen whether he likes it or not. Consequently, he must also realize, the time to replace lost business is before it is lost. The wise salesman seeks new customers *today,* no matter how well things are going, to replace the customers he is sure to lose tomorrow, next month or next year. If he does not, he is making one of the biggest— and most common—mistakes a salesman can make.

Because it often takes several months of hard work to develop a prospect and turn him into a regular account, *today* is never too early to think about the replacements that are sure to be needed in the future.

Let's take a closer look at this business of customer attrition to see some of the major reasons for it:

- A receptive buyer or purchasing agent is promoted, retires, or moves to another company, and is replaced by one with his own preferred suppliers.
- The customer firm goes out of business.
- The firm merges into a larger corporation that has its own sources of supply.
- The firm purchases a subsidiary company that produces the product it formerly bought on the outside.
- The customer firm changes its own product line, creating entirely new buying requirements.
- A new management demands change for the sake of change, and existing suppliers are summarily chopped off.

Whatever the reason or reasons at work in a given situation, Mr. Salesman is faced with the loss of what may be a sizable volume of business.

Now, many salesmen do recognize the ever-present possibilities of such customer loss. But all too often they fall into the trap of attempting to get in more solidly with their key customers and hoping against hope that "it" won't happen to them.

This is fine except for one thing—any accounts lost for the reasons mentioned above are lost for reasons that are far beyond the salesman's control. He may give the customer the best price and service available, but if that customer decides to merge, or is acquired by a larger outfit, or decides to change its product line, what's our salesman to do about it? About all he can do is go on a binge of self-consolation, reassuring himself that he did his best to hold the customer if this was at all possible.

But this consolation, needless to say, doesn't put orders in the book or dollars in the bank account.

How much more constructive it is to fight the battle offensively by insuring a steady supply of new accounts!

One of the most dramatic instances of this failure to anticipate the inevitable concerns an advertising man who for many years ran a highly successful agency with but three accounts.

Realizing that his sizable income stemmed from so few accounts, I had on many occasions urged him to devote even a small fraction of his time to soliciting new ones. But he inevitably gave the same excuses—he did not have the time; he could not afford the time; he could not take his attention away from his existing clients; his clients were all long-term accounts that were growing happier in their relationship with him year by year, and so forth.

Then I lost track of him for several years, until one not so fine day last year when I met him in Chicago and inquired how things were going. "George," he said, "you sure as shooting were right!" And he lost no time in telling me how he'd lost all three of his accounts.

One, a large shoe manufacturer, had been absorbed by a larger firm whose agency took over the account. This loss was made no more easy to bear by the explanation of the new management: One of the reasons they'd bought out his client, he was told, was because of the tremendous image he had created for its shoe line through his advertising efforts. They had paid the client company a handsome sum for this wonderful image, but they couldn't have two advertising agencies, and that was that.

His second client had suddenly become involved in a competitive rat race with foreign producers, and had been forced to cut expenditures to the bone. This meant cancellation of over a quarter of a million in advertising appropriations, with no hope that the budget would be reinstated for many years to come.

Loss of the third client presented perhaps the saddest story of all, since my friend had literally helped the company's president build the firm from the bottom up. But when the president's son took over, he had *his* own friends, and my friend lost out

Now all of this, almost incredibly, took place in less than a year. In twelve short months an established advertising business with billings of over $2 million literally hit the canvas—but hard.

Counterbalance Planned Ahead

The moral is here for any marketing man to grasp. In an increasingly complex and competitive economic world, it is no longer sufficient for a salesman to concentrate solely on the business he now regards as secure, though this is certainly important in its own right.

He must also, in full awareness of the law of attrition, make a deliberate and continuing effort to develop new customer accounts that will compensate—both in numbers and in sales dollars—for those accounts that will inevitably be lost through factors beyond his control.

This involves, of course, maintaining a constant lookout for likely prospects, researching the needs of such prospects, and making missionary-type calls from which he can generally expect no immediate sales return. Only through such advance prospecting can a salesman reasonably hope to provide the "pluses" that will counterbalance the "minuses" in his long-term ledger of accounts. Only in this way, in the final analysis, can he hope to keep himself and the firm he represents in the competitive race.

Unfortunately, however, many salesmen tend to look upon such missionary, or new account development, efforts as a waste of time merely because the same number of hours devoted to a customer already on the books will yield more here-and-now sales dollars. Add to this the fact that new account development is by no means an easy job (it is always easier to call upon existing customers whose needs are already known and with whom you feel quite comfortable), and you see why so many salesmen allow themselves to forget about new business when it isn't immediately needed.

A salesman just cannot afford to wait until the constantly eroding work of attrition eats away the very foundation of his income. By then it is often too late to make anything other than a frantic effort to pull in new business. And such last ditch efforts by an obviously desperate salesman are never conducive to the sort of psychology and approach needed to induce a prospect to commit his trust and his order.

When new accounts are needed least is also when the salesman can best afford the time for digging up new business. He can determine his own schedule, doing prospecting work without depriving his regular accounts. But, when the pressure builds and he must embark on a crash program for new business, neglect of other accounts is almost inevitable.

By going out after new accounts when there is little demand for increased sales volume, the salesman does not have to limit himself to just the biggest potential buyers. One of the most fertile grounds for new business is among the relatively small prospects that are often overlooked or neglected by the competition. With time on his side, the salesman can afford to develop those small-scale prospects that stand a good chance of paying off in big sales in the future. Indeed, I have known of salesmen who have built up phenomenal incomes through just such prospecting among small-growth companies which have turned into major accounts.

Sales management has a big responsibility in insuring a steady flow of new accounts. Before salesmen can be expected to set aside time for development when business is good, management must encourage and promote the practice. All too often when a salesman does realize the dangers presented by the law of attrition, he will be thwarted in his development efforts by a real or imagined company policy which overemphasizes immediate sales volume. Prospecting work is difficult and frustrating enough—without management's making it more so.

8

Forgetting the Rest of the Team

Is SELLING REALLY A PROFESSION?

All of us attend numerous sales conventions, meetings and seminars every year. Inevitably, some speaker will bring up this question of the professional status of selling. Just as inevitably, the speaker will conclude that selling is a profession, and will support his theory by citing the higher levels of education required in many selling jobs today, the never-ending training that salesmen receive on the job, the "codes of ethics" that many companies have formulated for their salesmen, and so on.

Now, I am perfectly willing to admit that such factors bode well for the future of selling. But I seriously doubt that these factors, in and of themselves, are the requisites for what would be called professional status. Something more must be added. And that something is a sense of obligation—or a conscience—toward the other persons with whom the true professional deals.

The doctor must bear a decided sense of duty to his patients. The lawyer must have a similar relationship with his clients, the teacher with his pupils, and so on.

At this point many a salesman would be quick to agree—and

to point to his unswerving loyalty to the customer as evidence of his own professionalism.

So far, no argument.

But this is only half the story. The other half—the half that is too often missing—has to do with the salesman's sense of obligation toward another and much larger group of people. Without this no salesman can truly call himself a professional.

Who are these other persons? They are the men and women "back at the ranch"—the production workers, the engineers and scientists, the designers, the accountants, the shipping clerks, the secretaries, the elevator operators, the guards, the managers, etc., who produce and deliver the products that the salesman attempts to sell.

Only to the extent that the salesman has their interests at heart does he function as a true professional in the field of selling.

Self-Interest Overrated

What, after all, really motivates a salesman to put forth his best effort in every selling situation? Some might say the answer is plain old self-interest, the desire to earn more and more income. But there is good reason to doubt the validity of this answer.

When it comes to income potentials, the overwhelming majority of salesmen seem *not* to be shooting for the top. Otherwise they'd be giving a lot more time, energy, and intelligence to their selling tasks. Such salesmen—and their numbers are far too great in what is supposedly a dynamic economy—are content with a fair-to-average expenditure of effort and with the fair-to-average income level thus produced. In other words, they become "comfortable" and stop striving.

One time, several of us were on a weekend fishing trip. One of the group, a salesman, mentioned several times a big call he was to make on Monday. Then, on Sunday night, he announced that he was going to stay over at the lodge another day. "But what about that important call, Art?" we asked. He replied, in effect, that "the commission on this deal won't be more than $100 or $150 and, frankly, I'd rather go fishing. The extra day is worth that to me."

Now Art, in fact, didn't need the money. He had done pretty well in the market, and he was a fairly good salesman who earned a better-than-average income. But where was Art's sense of professional obligation (and he would have referred to himself as a professional) toward the several hundred employees who made up the company he represented? What about the production workers, for example, to whom that sales order would have indirectly meant added job security? As a matter of fact, this happened at a time when the firm was having to lay off some of its plant people because of slack business.

And what about the other employees whose livelihoods, chances for promotion, hopes for salary increases, and so forth would be affected—infinitesimally, perhaps, but they would be affected none the less!

What, for that matter, about the stockholder owners of the firm? Multiplied many times over, this sort of selling laxity would certainly color the income statements they would be honored with at the end of the fiscal year. And let's not forget the customer himself. Would he be as receptive in the future to my salesman friend, or to any other representative of this firm?

Obvious questions, yes. But how many salesmen actually think of such factors when exhibiting such lax salesmanship? How many, in short, possess the sort of conscience that's needed to translate selling into a real professional calling?

Yet any sales manager can recite from his own experience numerous case histories similar to the one outlined above— histories of salesmen who lack any sense of responsibility toward those whose economic fate they determine.

It might be added that such salesmen seldom realize their

full potentials or graduate into the top ranks of star performers. Because they function from a narrow and essentially selfish point of view, they automatically block out a vital area of self-motivation.

Impact of the Invisible Critic

One of the most truly professional salesmen I have ever met, a man we shall call Ed, uses this approach: When he's about to make an important sales call, Ed frequently imagines his presentation will be observed by an audience of 200 or so persons from his own company. "I try to give the best possible performance for their benefit," he notes, "almost as though I were an actor on a stage and wanted very much to win their approval and their applause. And after every such presentation, I go back and review my performance honestly, trying to determine where it could have been better, sharper, more effective, etc."

Almost as if to summarize this approach, Ed adds: "The salesman, in the final analysis, doesn't produce a product. Nor does he research, develop, design, engineer, ship, or service it. He is, by contrast, the one man representative of a total operation. And for the time that he stands in the prospect's or customer's office, he literally holds the destiny of that whole organization in his hands."

Now, a salesman like Ed is clearly motivated to a far greater extent than most salesmen today. He is motivated by factors outside the immediate range of his self-interest, by the knowledge that the well-being of others depends, to at least some degree, on the quality of his performance.

This is a state of mind, it hardly needs to be pointed out, that characterizes most true professionals, regardless of the nature of their occupation. It is the state of mind that motivates a man to give more than other men might give under similar conditions, that keeps him striving for top performance in his every act and effort. And such a man, in the long run, reaps many returns denied to those who lack this sense of obligation. He is the salesman who wins the recognition and respect, even the affection, of everyone in his organization. And in keeping their interests in mind, he also serves his own best interests. For he is the salesman who rises to the top and stays there.

At this point, many a salesman might wonder about the other side of this relationship. "What support do I get," he asks, "from those who supposedly back me up?" He goes on to recite examples of how production, or shipping, or credit, or service, or what have you, loused him up in a given sales situation.

The answer is simple. The salesman who operates as a professional inevitably wins the respect and full cooperation of the men and women who make up his company. He should, of course, tak every opportunity to let them know that his selling conscience is operative—that he is guided by a larger perspective which includes the well-being of all whose efforts contribute to the product or service that he sells.

9

Overlooking the Value of "Dry-Run" Calls

AT A RECENT COCKTAIL PARTY, A PROMINENT ACTOR WAS asked why he had accepted a role in a little-known summer stock company (at an infinitesimal salary) immediately after completing a grueling but highly successful Broadway season.

"It's all very simple," he explained. "Summer stock gives me an opportunity to practice and polish my work. And, if I make any mistakes in the course of some innovation or experimentation, there won't be any sophisticated audiences or Broadway critics taking me apart for it."

He went on to say that no really professional actor ever makes the mistake of being fully satisfied with his performance, or fails to experiment—where it doesn't count—with new techniques or innovations in style.

The same is true of salesmen. Yet, how many go on, year after year, satisfied with their technique and mistakenly failing to experiment or innovate?

The salesman, of course, has no "summer stock." But he does have an ideal opportunity for "practice where it doesn't count" in the "dry-run" presentation: the sales call on the small and relatively unimportant prospect from whom he really does not expect to obtain an order.

Such dry runs offer advantages that shouldn't be overlooked by any salesman, whether he is just beginning his career or has already established his reputation as a star performer. Let's take a look at a few of these advantages:

. . . Practice for the Big Ones

Few salesmen will deny that practice makes perfect. But far too many seem to think that practice sessions can be limited to standing before a mirror and acting out their sales presentation. Many sales managers seem to err here too—treating role playing as the ultimate form of sales practice, and forgetting that practice, in fact, has many dimensions.

Yet what better form of practice is there—for neophyte or veteran salesman—than to actually make a sales presentation to a prospect who, figuratively, "doesn't count." Here is the ideal opportunity for the salesman to relax, to almost sit back and watch himself in action. Not being concerned about an order, he can afford to do this. And the resulting improvement that such practice produces pays dividends later when he makes the critical calls from which he does hope to obtain orders.

. . . A Chance to Improvise

Rare is the salesman who doesn't at one time or another feel that a change in his selling method might produce better results. But just as rare is the salesman who actually experiments with such changes. Why? Because most of them are afraid of trying something new that might cost them an important sale. It's easy to stick with what we're used to and which has worked pretty well in the past, and is known to be safe.

With a dry-run presentation, however, the salesman doesn't have to worry about being safe. Since he doesn't really expect to make a sale, what can he lose by a bit of experimentation? Here is the chance for the salesman to exhibit some of that creativity he so often complains he must stifle. And if it seems to work, he's so much the richer. Who knows but what the selling innovation the salesman tries during a dry run today may—with practice and polish—become his key to many sales successes tomorrow.

. . . Opportunity for Appraisals

No salesman is well advised to wind up a presentation to an important prospect or customer by asking, "How am I doing?" In the case of a dry run, however, it's possible to do just that. And it's both surprising and gratifying to discover the number of prospects and customers who are willing to give a frank appraisal of a salesman's performance, discuss their reactions, and make suggestions.

Sometimes during dry runs the salesmen can go out in pairs —one to make the presentation, the other to watch and later report his reactions. In the course of several such dry-run situations, two men can build up quite accurate appraisals of one another's selling performance. Using two men in this manner gives this dry run an added dimension, and any sales manager might do well to consider teaming up two salesmen for at least a few such calls.

. . . A Needed Warm-up

A salesman has an 11 A.M. appointment with a major prospect or customer. Anxious to be as well prepared and mentally ready as possible, he has several cups of coffee, studies his material, rearranges his samples, reads a magazine or two, has a few more cups of coffee, etc. To a certain extent, this works—but it might have worked better if he'd used these few hours to dry-run his presentation on someone else.

Who else? It doesn't really matter, just so long as it places him in a situation somewhat similar to the one he's about to face. Maybe he can set up such a dry-run appointment in advance. And there's no reason why he can't just walk into any nearby plant or office building and make a cold call on almost any possible "prospect."

The important thing is that such a warm-up presentation can literally melt away inner tensions and fears. Not unlike a boxer's shadow boxing in the ring, or a pitcher's warm-up in the bull pen, this dry run assures the salesman of peak performance during his actual meeting with the customer.

The dry run, in other words, provides a wonderful and exciting opportunity for the salesman to practice, experiment or warm up—before a live audience.

The dry run can give other, secondary benefits, too. Although its main purpose is not to create immediate sales but to develop selling skills, there will be occasions where the dry run produces more immediate results. For example, the dry-run prospect sometimes proves able to place an order—generally, much to the salesman's surprise. Many times, too, such calls result in valuable sales leads which the dry-run prospect gladly passes along to the salesman. Indeed, these small-timers are often so delighted that a salesman will take the time and trouble to call on them that they make a personal effort to suggest other firms that might be contacted profitably.

Nor should any salesman forget this important fact: The target of today's dry run may be small indeed, but small businesses may eventually grow and prosper. And the salesman who made his contacts during the early stage may be well received and regarded in future years.

Dry-run calls, by the way, need not be one-shot affairs. There are salesmen who make call after call on the same dry-run prospect. Again, they don't do this with any idea of making a sale, but rather for the progressively more valuable experience such repeat calls afford. One veteran salesman put it this way: "You know, I often call on my big accounts five or more times before getting the particular order I'm shooting for. And each of these calls is essentially different, since each time I'm building on what I said, did, promised or what have you during each of my preceding calls. So, when it comes to dry-run situations, I do the same thing, going back to the same firm time after time, trying to learn as much as I can about my reactions and the prospect's reactions. This gives me a lot of insight and ideas I can use when I try to hook the really big fish."

Speaking of veteran salesmen, let me add this: A salesman may reach the point in his career when he no longer practices before a mirror several mornings each week, or when he feels that role playing is something for the younger men just getting into selling. But no salesman ever reaches the stage where he can afford to make the mistake of underrating the kind of experience gained in a dry-run call.

10

Ignoring the Buying "Influentials"

IT WAS THE DAY THE YOUNG SALESMAN HAD BEEN WAITING for. It brought the opportunity to make his sales presentation to the company vice president. And this man, the salesman knew, might place an initial order in excess of $80,000.

Technically, the presentation could not have been more ideal. Psychologically, it was a disaster.

For this salesman had taken the vice president for what he, quite literally, seemed to be—a man of considerable personal power and decisiveness. Accordingly, the young man focused 99 and 99/100 per cent of his attention directly upon his prospect. The remaining 1/100 per cent—in the form of an occasional side glance—he had given to the third party present, a rather timid looking individual whom the vice president had introduced as ". . . one of our plant engineers, Jim B . . ." (The salesman hadn't even caught the last name!)

And to whom does the dynamic, chin-jutting vice president turn for an opinion—indeed, for a decision—at the conclusion of the presentation? He turns directly to this Casper Milquetoast of an engineer. And what does Mr. Engineer do? He turns thumbs down on the whole idea. In short, No Sale.

This story has always touched home with me; in fact, I happen to have been the young salesman involved. That was a good many years ago, of course. But the incident showed me a vital mistake still made by thousands of salesmen today; *overlooking the "influentials"—the men who influence the key decision maker—in a sales situation.*

This is a lesson, call it a moral if you prefer, all the more important today when the salesman increasingly finds himself faced with a "buying audience" rather than a single decision maker. As one veteran salesman recently expressed it, "It was hard enough selling to the judge. But now my prospects bring so many people into the room it's like having to sell to the jury as well!"

Moreover, it's a mistake that's easier to make these days, when salesmen are hounded and implored to "go to the top" with the sales presentation. And often company rank is confused with true buying influence.

Who Are the "Influentials"?

Even where the salesman faces only a single decision maker, the power of the influentials may loom in the background. Nor is there anything untoward about this. The prospect or customer, being only human, wants to make the right buying decision—and for this reason he respects the counsel, requested or volunteered, of others in his organization. And these others can range from his #1 assistant to the receptionist in the outer office.

The influential, in short, can be anyone who happens to have the buyer's ear and whose opinions he happens to value—particularly as regards the salesman and the product the salesman wants to sell him.

I remember the day when, as a young child living in Brooklyn, I saw the Cadillac salesman come "calling" on my dad with a bright new model. Dad, despite his previous interests in

this car, couldn't quite make up his mind. But did that salesman waste a moment arguing the advantages of his product?
Not a one. He just looked at me, my brother, and my sister and
said "How 'bout it kids? Let's take a ride." And ride we did,
while our chauffeur-salesman—whom we'd by that time equated
with Santa Claus—casually drew attention to every feature of
that Cadillac which would appeal to a child.

When we drove back about an hour later, Dad didn't have
a chance. And we kids did all the selling. That was one salesman,
be sure, who knew the value as well as the meaning of influentials.

In attempting to correct one mistake, however, salesmen sometimes make another. Not everyone involved in a buying situation will actually prove to be an influential. Usually only one
or two people exert the sort of influence that can swing the buying decision one way or the other. These are the people the
salesman must quickly spot, and towards whom he must direct
at least a portion of his selling energies.

How does he do this? How does the salesman "uncover"
the influentials who surround the key decision maker? Here
are some guidelines that may be of help to the men in the
field:

The salesman must of necessity sharpen his powers of observation, particularly if he expects to find himself faced not by
a single individual but by a group—a plant manager (perhaps
the key decision maker), a department head, one or more
engineers, etc. Here the salesman must learn to automatically
ask and find the answers to a number of questions: To whom
does the key decision maker seem to defer? Which of these other
men speaks up most readily and/or most confidentially? Which
man asks the most critical questions? Which seems to have the
most information regarding the need for the product to be
purchased, the nature of the product(s) that can fill this need,
and so forth?

Obviously it is not always easy for the salesman, particularly
if he is inexperienced, to concentrate on these questions while

at the same time trying to move ahead with his presentation. But here again it is a matter of practice making perfect, and after not too long a time this sort of situational probing can become almost intuitive. There's no black magic involved, just sheer practice in looking for the underlying clues that point to this man or that as the influential who must be carefully nurtured during the course of the selling presentation.

The Waiting Game

Delay can also be an important aid in sensing the influential. All too many salesmen jump too quickly into what might be called the formal phase of the selling presentation. The skilled salesman, by contrast, plays a waiting game. He keeps the situation on as informal a basis as possible until such time as he uncovers clues which point to the influential. He keeps the conversation on as light a level as possible while he probes the relationships among those whom he faces.

One of the best ways to uncover the buying influential—and oddly enough one of the most neglected—is to openly question each individual introduced into the situation. Thus the salesman might ask, "And what exactly, sir, does your job encompass?" . . "Could you please clear me up on the reasons for your participation in this meeting?" or even a frank "What role will you play in the final decision?"

Blunt questions, yes. But properly placed and toned, they need not appear blunt. And in a surprising number of instances, they will receive surprisingly direct and honest answers. Even where the individual may hedge in his answers, the salesman can, by careful observation, gain a clearer insight into the degree of influence represented by each person.

Pre-Meeting Check

Where the salesman has some idea of the persons who will be

present during the buying situation, he is always well advised to make a pre-meeting check. Thus he might contact other individuals he happens to know in the prospect or customer firm, and ask their opinion as to the relative influence of, say, Mr. X. Or, lacking such internal contacts, he might seek the opinions of those in other companies, in trade associations, etc., who might have "a line" on Mr. X. Indeed, in some instances the prospect's own secretarv can be the richest source of the desired information—if not, in actual fact, an influential in her own right.

This before-the-meeting check is especially vital, of course, where the salesman makes his presentation to a single individual but knows the final decision must wait upon consultations with one or more influentials in that firm. Learning who these influentials happen to be enables him to include in his presentation the types of material to which they will react most positively. And many a sale has been won because the salesman made direct or indirect contact with such behind-the-scenes influentials before and/or following his actual presentation.

One word of caution might be advisable. Many a salesman, having successfully learned to spot the influential, tends to over-direct his presentation to this individual. What he forgets, of course, is that the influential is so called precisely because he exerts an influence on a "primary mover," whom we have called the key decision maker.

Any manager pointing out the need to sell the influential must stress that this requires a carefully balanced approach aimed at selling one man without unselling or offending another. Many times this will involve addressing the key decision maker, but with words and ideas that are really aimed at the influential who sits at his side. This is a skill, to be sure, that takes a while to acquire; but it is the sort of practice that pays off in profits.

11

The Mistake of Fearing a Prospect

A FOOTBALL COACH OR BASEBALL MANAGER IS PAID TO prejudge or second guess the opposition. He knows how the game is played and the potentiality of the other team. If he's an astute leader, his prejudging often pays off.

The salesman who attempts the same technique in prejudging a prospect is headed for trouble. Chances are he'll guess wrong and lose the order.

Why? The football coach is dealing with simple strategy. He prepares a defense to counter an expected offense. He is not concerned with the subtleties of human nature.

The salesman, however, is dealing with the human element. He knows that his job is to overcome the buyer's opposition and sell his product. But, in so doing, the salesman creates imaginary boogy men. He defeats himself.

The Myth of the Monolithic Buyer

How? By wrongly prejudging his prospect. He creates in his mind the image of an all-powerful, omnipotent buyer. He is afraid. He magnifies his difficulties, putting himself in a subservient position. The prospect is a terrifying obstacle to over-come. It's unlikely that the salesman will make it. He is crawl-ing up a mountain, convinced he will never reach the top.

This salesman's problem should be obvious by now: he lacks self-confidence. He is letting the prospect call the shot, although the salesman may be the more informed man.

The salesman must keep in mind that the prospect is a human being. He is beset by the same doubts, fears and frustrations that plague all of us. For this reason, he may take advantage of a situation that makes him number one. Let a timid, unsure salesman walk into his office and the buyer will exploit that advantage. Perhaps it satisfies his ego to keep the salesman off balance and afraid.

A friend of mine spent a number of years in Europe as a cor-respondent for a world-wide news service. One day he managed to get an interview with Mussolini at the height of the Italian dictator's power. Now my friend, Bill Roark, had been around. He had interviewed numerous big-name people in various fields. In so doing, he had acquired a fairly competent knowl-edge of human nature. He wasn't easily impressed. But even Bill was not prepared for Mussolini. After taking an elevator to the fourth floor of Il Duce's headquarters, my friend had to walk about 250 feet through a cathedral-like room toward the Great Man, who was seated behind an enormous desk. The shadowed chamber gave the whole experience a dreamlike quality. Bill, a hard-bitten, experienced newspaperman, was actually trembling as he approached Mussolini.

"It was an experience I'll never forget," Bill told me.

But he also realized later that the reception was all part of a plan. Mussolini was no fool. He realized the psychological ad-vantage in such a situation. He knew the average visitor would finally arrive at his desk thoroughly cowed by the ordeal. From then on, it was easy for the dictator to dominate the interview.

But suppose the guest had been smart enough to speculate that perhaps Mussolini was, in reality, a frightened, insecure individual and that he employed these stage props to compensate for his weakness. How easy it would have been for the visitor to seize the initiative in the meeting.

Capitalize on Your Expertise

There is a lesson here for the salesman. Instead of magnifying the prospect's power, knowledge and authority, the salesman should consider his own side of the ledger. He should tell himself: "I'm the expert here. I don't care how big or important the prospect is. I know my product thoroughly and my company is standing behind me. I'm actually in a position to help this buyer and, given a chance, I'll tell him so." The salesman can make his point without getting smart or offensive. All he has to do is radiate confidence and knowledge.

I can put it another way. The salesman must have the courage of his convictions; in short, old-fashioned guts.

Don't Undermine Yourself with Groundless Fears

Your reasoning powers should warn you against useless worrying. An example comes to mind in a recent interview I had with a job applicant. The man was extremely nervous and I wanted to put him at ease.

"Look, John," I said, "I'm only acting for a client. My mind is completely open on your application. Just relax and I'll hear you out completely. It might help you to realize that our positions could have been reversed. It's just the way breaks come."

I really got to that man. He unwound in a moment, made a brilliant case for himself, and got the job.

But think of the senseless agony. He probably had spent a sleepless night thinking of the interview and was sweating with fear and self-doubt when it came.

Rather than throw away the pre-interview period in fruitless guessing and imagining, concentrate instead on *your* presentation or, if that doesn't work, erase the whole matter from your mind temporarily.

A chauffeur used to drive me to my appointments. Between these engagements, I forced myself to lean back in the car and put my mind completely out of focus. I blanked out my thinking so I would form no prejudgments about my next visit. Odds are that the prospect or customer is ready to receive you with an open mind. He isn't going to refuse you an order because you have blue eyes or a grey suit. He simply wants to know what you can do for him and his company. If he tries to throw his weight around, let him. But don't let it rattle you. Your weight lies in your knowledge and confidence in your product, your experience and your conviction that you are there to be heard.

Keep in mind that prejudging is usually wrong judging. You have a tough enough job in selling your product. Don't make the job any tougher.

12

Underutilizing Your Own Resources

WALT ANDERSON, A CHEMICAL PRODUCTS SALESMAN, thought he had it made. He was 38 years old, made $12,000 a year, and had a pretty wife, two fine kids and a pleasant home. He covered the southeastern states for an Ohio firm that was number two or three in its field. His boss liked him and he liked his job.

You Must Grow with Your Product and Company

Walt's blissful state might have continued indefinitely but for a chance meeting on a plane flying from Baltimore to Richmond. His seatmate happened to be a chemical engineer who was familiar with Walt's company.

"You know," the man remarked, "your outfit has really come up fast in the last ten years. There's been a 100 percent improvement in your product."

The comment triggered a thought process that jolted Walt out of his serenity. By the time the plane landed he had done a lot of thinking about himself and his organization.

The 10-year figure was the key to Walt's reflections. His firm had made spectacular strides but had he kept pace in those 10 years? The only honest answer was "no."

He knew in his heart that his personal progress did not match his company's advances in product improvement, engineering, distribution and prestige. He had been content to ride along on the firm's coattails.

Like many other salesmen, Walt made the mistake of not taking inventory of himself or keeping a performance record of his personal attributes which mean so much in selling.

All companies take periodic inventories to find out what they've got, what they need, and what they want to eliminate. A salesman should take personal stock for the same reason. He must identify his weak and strong points, decide where improvements should be made and get rid of bad habits that kill sales.

Honestly Reappraise Yourself

However, self-appraisal is useless if the man is not completely honest with himself. This is not the time for self-deception.

Walt Anderson took inventory of himself by drawing a parallel with his company's expansion. He came in a poor second. He next mapped out a personal performance rating sheet that served as a systematic guide to his progress. He listed such qualities as honesty, dependability, resourcefulness, patience, confidence, cheerfulness, appearance, dress, sincerity, style, willingness to learn, initiative, and knowledge of his company's product line, practices, and policies.

He established 100 as a perfect score and 70 as passing. If he flubbed a presentation because he misjudged a prospect, he gave himself a low mark for judgment. If he cracked a tough holdout after 25 calls his patience and persistence standings rose sharply. Of course, a rating chart is valueless if the salesman does nothing about his low scores. Walt concentrated on raising his marks until he had progressed on every point.

Walt began the rating ledger five years ago. Since that time he has become one of the top earners in his outfit. His sales manager was so impressed with his idea that he drew up and distributed a similar chart for all his salesmen.

Your Most Important Asset

Shortly after I learned about Walt's system I met him at a Cleveland sales meeting.

"What did you really discover from all this?" I asked him.

Walt took a thoughtful drag on a cigarette and replied: "The main thing I found out is that my most important asset is myself. I've got a good company behind me and a high quality product but so have my competitors. It's the impression a salesman makes on a customer that means the difference between leaving with an order or empty-handed."

I've never heard a better description of selling. The man who wants to push ahead must figuratively put himself under a microscope to enlarge his flaws.

Once these mistakes are exposed they can be analyzed and eradicated.

Some of you may ask: "If this rating business is so great why don't more salesmen use it?"

Because they haven't got the guts. It takes raw courage for a man to admit his drawbacks. Many marriages break up because neither husband nor wife will admit they were wrong. An alcoholic won't face his problem, preferring to think of himself as a "social drinker." A motorist risks death or injury rather than concede the other guy might have the right-of-way.

The world is full of people who refuse to admit their shortcomings. They take refuge in cozy excuses and downright lying.

This attitude is particularly damaging to the salesman. He works alone. He is not a member of a "team operation" whereby if he drops the ball somebody else will pick it up. He must recover his own fumbles and even those of others. If a customer is dissatisfied it's the salesman who usually hears about it first.

That's why it is so important that the salesman structure his character through some form of self-evaluation. He'll still get his lumps from time to time but not nearly as often as the man who makes no attempt to improve himself.

Polish Up Your Personal Performance

Self-rating changed Jeff Kingman from a plodding hack to a sparkling salesman. Jeff, who sold industrial floor wax, did not grasp the importance of the suggestion technique. Surveys prove that suggestions lift sales averages from 30 to 100 percent, but he never connected the evidence to his own territory and remained a low producer.

His interviews lacked imagination. He neglected to suggest benefits from the product nor took any pains to fire the prospect's interest. It would not have occurred to him to suggest an additional purchase after making a sale. He was so exalted by his one breakthrough that he was only too happy to fold up his tent and steal away.

"Why push my luck?" he told himself.

One day Jeff got a blunt warning from his boss.

"You're not producing," the sales manager said. "You're hitting only about 3 percent of the potential in your territory while our competitors are knocking down 60 percent."

That woke Jeff up. He knew the next time he was called in would be the last.

He talked it over with his wife, Helen, that night.

"Darling," she said, "you remember that last week I took Bobby to the doctor for his annual checkup?"

"Yes," Jeff answered, "but what does that have to do with my situation?"

"Well," Helen went on, "Dr. Ames keeps a record of Bobby's physical development, a kind of performance chart. Each year he's expected to grow at a certain rate. If he doesn't there may be something wrong."

"But," Jeff persisted, "I still don't see what our son has. . . ."

"Wait a minute," Helen cut in. "I was just thinking that you might fix up some sort of performance chart to tell how you're growing on your job."

Helen had struck home. An idea began boiling in Jeff's head.

The next day he marched into the sales manager's office and asked point blank:

"What do you consider my greatest weakness?"

His superior was equally direct.

"You're not aggressive enough."

Driving to his calls that afternoon, Jeff took inventory of himself and came to the same conclusion. He spent the following weekend working up a chart to measure his performance each month. He began by giving himself a zero for aggressiveness. Jeff had nowhere to go but up.

And he went up. It was hard at first to change his comfortable routine but he did it.

When a prospect hesitated, Jeff made specific suggestions to arouse his interest. In seeking interviews he kindled desire by mentioning special benefits he offered. He got more interviews and more orders. After one year he could honestly give himself a score of 100 on aggressiveness.

He told me recently:

"Maybe I could have done it without the rating gimmick, but I don't think so. I had to dump a lot of bad habits, that's true. But I got a real bang out of seeing my score jump each month. It gave me something to shoot for."

Self-Evaluation Helps You to Find Hidden Potential

The best thing about the self-rating process is that it usually digs out qualities the salesman never realized he possessed. He gets to know himself and what he can really do if he tries.

Another advantage is that a personal inventory and subsequent control are a form of self-management. The salesman, probably more than anyone, must learn to manage his own development. Help can come from his boss and others but in the final showdown it is the man himself who is responsible for his success or failure.

The man who gets backed into a corner by a prospect can't reach for the book or phone his company. He's got to get out himself. If he knows his capabilities he will have found a way to shift gear and get on top of the situation.

One of the finest salesmen I know, Roy Liddell, once had trouble recalling names and facts involved in his calls. He whipped up a memory jogger that tracked his progress in that area. Then, right after each contact, he made detailed notes that enabled him to return to the prospect armed with all the necessary data.

Another top salesman, Harvey Rogers, doublechecks his own estimation of his performance by frankly asking the prospect's opinion of his sales talk. The results are worth the momentary embarrassment.

Harvey, who handles power tools, once invited a purchasing agent's opinion of the way he showed his application.

"Lousy," the man retorted. He explained that the salesman's approach revealed little understanding of the firm's needs.

Harvey, who keeps score on himself, flunked "customer understanding" that month but the experience spurred him to better interview preparation. He boned up on that firm's requirements until he knew them inside out. The next time he saw the same prospect he came through with a brilliant application showing that won him a big order.

High producers have never been afraid to dispassionately examine themselves for weak spots. They meet their problems squarely, not by retreating into a never-never-land of self-deception. They have learned the importance of personal inventory and the constant need for self-criticism.

In salesmanship there is only one payoff—making sales. To score in this department you have to know yourself and realize your maximum potential.

Don't be afraid of the knowledge. It's your key to success.

13

Trying to Sell without
Customer Knowledge

A PROFESSIONAL FOOTBALL COACH WOULDN'T DREAM OF sending his team into action without a thorough knowledge of his opposition. Both sides scout each other's games. Movies of the opponent's previous contests are viewed as many as 150 times by players and coaches. The competition's weak and strong points are shrewdly analyzed. By kickoff time the coach knows almost as much about his rivals as his own club. This kind of information has won many gridiron battles.

The salesman's battle can be won by his knowledge of the customer. The man who devotes time and effort in gathering data about the buyer can write his own ticket. Such labor means the difference between the order taker and the true salesman. The former is running on a treadmill; the latter is going places.

Research Your Customers

The salesman who yearns for higher earnings should diligently research his customers and make the information a part of his presentation.

Barney Ashmore, a top-drawer paper products salesman, invited my wife and me to his home for bridge one night. After the game I remembered that Barney had the address of a mutual friend I wanted to contact. Barney took me into a room he had converted into an office. While he searched for the address, I gazed around. The room bulged with filing cabinets.

"You have almost as many file cases as I have in my downtown office," I remarked. "What do you keep in them—scrapbooks of your triumphs?"

My friend laughed.

"Well," he replied, "some hold my bookkeeping records and company material, but most of them contain personal and business information about my customers. Let me show you."

He slid open a case and pulled at random a folder on the "Z" Company and its officers. I had never seen such an exhaustive dossier. The history, organization, earning record, credit rating and future plans of the firm were recorded in minute detail. Also noted were the company's policies on distribution, sales, advertising, and merchandising and purchasing.

And if that weren't enough, Barney had also listed the company's problems, routines, and procedures. There was even a routing map of the most efficient way to get there. Also recorded were facts on how Barney's product will be used.

In addition, there was a complete rundown on each executive—his likes, dislikes, quirks, hobbies, family, age, background, schooling, political leanings, reputation, daily routine, and club memberships.

There was even a note of where the man spent his vacations.

Also in the folder were annual company reports from five years back. Barney explained that he bought one share of stock in each of his customer firms to keep abreast of its earnings and prospects.

"All this must have taken years to accumulate," I said.

"It was worth it," Barney asserted. "These firms are my meal ticket. They will send my kids to college and pay my mortgage. Why shouldn't I take time to learn about them?"

The More Facts, the Better the Presentation

Barney made good sense. A common mistake of salesmen is that they don't realize the power in knowledge. They are dazzled by the success stories of other salesmen without realizing that these men gave something extra to their jobs. The high-income salesmen learned long ago that the more they know about the prospect, the more effective will be their presentation.

Barney walks into a buyer's office armed with hundreds of facts, both important and trivial—yet all are relative to the man and the company he is trying to sell. He has done his homework so thoroughly that he is a veritable encyclopedia of information. Often he can supply a purchasing agent with data about the firm that the man didn't know himself. For this reason, many buyers think of Barney as a valuable consultant.

Compare Barney with the salesman who doesn't understand the importance of selling research. This man seeks success by wining and dining his customers to the neglect of his family. He relies on a smooth line of patter that is empty of hard facts. He looks for shortcuts. Somehow he thinks orders will drop on him like manna from heaven if only he is a nice guy and keeps his clothes pressed. This type of salesman won't starve, but he'll never make the big leagues either. He is doomed to mediocrity, to hitting a plateau early in his career and staying there. What he doesn't realize is that the Barneys also are nice guys, wear neat suits, and have the *added* advantage of customer knowledge.

Sources of General Information on the Customer

There are many ways to learn about your customers. The

newspapers, business journals, trade papers, and magazines are good sources. Some salesmen subscribe to a clipping service that furnishes them with social as well as business items from the media.

It certainly won't hurt your cause if you mention casually to a customer: "Oh, by the way, I saw the picture and announcement of your daughter's engagement in the paper. She certainly is a lovely girl."

Your company can also supply you with valuable information about your prospects and territory.

A prime source is the customer himself. People like to talk about themselves and buyers are no exception. Perhaps only a word or two is needed to draw him out about his family, golf score or basement workshop. If you don't know much about golf or turret lathes, find out. Plenty of good books are available on these subjects. Read them so that the next time you'll be able to talk the customer's language.

Even the time spent waiting to see a prospect can be utilized in research. Talk to his secretary. She may feed you valuable tips. These gals know quite a bit about their bosses.

Systematize the Facts You Find

However the information is collected, a catalogue system should be worked out. The method will often depend on the salesman himself, his work habits, available time and facilities. But the data should become part of his permanent record at the first opportunity, otherwise it may be forgotten.

Mel Thomas, a plumbing supply salesman, keeps one set of files in his home and a duplicate set in his car. This allows him to quickly review important facts at lunch or between calls. He has another reason for the twin sets.

"I put 15 years of work into those records," Mel told me once. "I'd be sunk if they were ever destroyed by fire or accident. The extra set protects me against the possibility."

Advantages of Cataloguing

Some data may have no immediate value but are kept for future use. An insurance salesman, for example, keeps track of a young man on the way up. One day he reads in the paper that the man has been promoted to a top executive position at a possible $15,000 raise in salary. The salesman can safely assume the prospect is in the market for more insurance.

Joe Marsh, a lumber salesman, learns that T. W. Harkness, purchasing agent for the ABC furniture factory, has moved to the XYZ firm, a competitive outfit.

The salesman checks his records and finds out that Harkness liked his product but felt that shipping costs were prohibitive and didn't buy. The XYZ company is much closer to Marsh's mill so he makes a note to call on Harkness at his first opportunity.

Prospect facts also save time and trouble for the salesman. His information helps eliminate wasted calls and callbacks on unproductive customers.

Another point to remember is that buyer knowledge gives the salesman the edge in an interview. The customer is flattered and impressed by the seller who has a sure grasp of his problems. He can see that the salesman has invested time, energy and perhaps money in familiarizing himself with the firm's circumstances. The salesman has *earned* the right to be heard.

And the salesman can get right down to the business of selling. There is no need to take up his or the prospect's time in probing for facts he has already. Also, when questions are hurled at him, the salesman doesn't have to fumble around for answers or admit his ignorance. Vital data can be delivered at a moment's notice.

It should be pointed out here that knowledge of his own product and company are equally important to the salesman in his presentation.

Forearmed with this mass of information, he can talk in concrete terms, avoiding vague generalities and platitudes.

Your Knowledge Can Help the Customer

Today we think of the salesman as a friend and adviser to his customer. He helps him with merchandising ideas, promotion and displays. He even gives financial counsel. The seller best equipped to give all this aid is the one who has studied and researched the customer so sweepingly that he can actually put himself in the latter's place.

This reminds me of Frank Wilson, a floor covering salesman and close friend of mine. One day at lunch I was introduced to one of Frank's biggest customers.

"Frank always amazes me," the man said. "He knows as much about my business as I do myself. He can come into my place and put his finger right on my particular problem.

"What's more, he comes up with the answer."

In my book, this is one of the highest compliments you can pay a salesman. Frank lives in a $60,000 home. His son attends one of the best eastern schools and two years ago he and his family spent three months in Europe.

Frank learned long ago that customers aren't bowled over by slick conversation, a flashy personality or a whirlwind approach. They want sympathetic understanding of their problems and an assurance that the salesman's advice and counsel are based on sound knowledge.

It's a mistake to think there is a shortcut to this knowledge. A salesman acquires it through hard work, diligence and a strong desire for success.

14

Going Over the Buyer's Head

The Immovable Object

EVERY SALESMAN RUNS INTO AT LEAST ONE BUYER HE can't budge.

No matter how hard he tries, he can't get to first base with the man.

After a while the seller says to himself: "My presentation was sound and my product is good. It must be that the buyer is either stubborn or stupid, or both."

This is usually when the salesman starts thinking of going over the buyer's head. In 99 out of 100 cases he should count to 10 and then not do it. Bypassing the buyer is a mistake that can ruin the salesman with that company and possibly his own.

In the first place, the man upstairs will probably bounce him right back to the purchasing agent. In running to the agent's boss, the salesman has, in effect, questioned the firm's judgment in appointing that buyer. Management doesn't like to be told that it has goofed. Therefore, the salesman will be told:

"Take it up with Mr. Jones. That's why we have him on our staff."

An Embarrassing Position

This puts the salesman in the embarrassing position of having to retrace his steps to Jones, the buyer, who will be, probably, even more adamant than before. He certainly won't thank you for trying to make him look bad.

Can you blame either him or management?

Supposing that a customer went over your head to complain about an order. Wouldn't you be angry and resentful? And wouldn't you expect your management to kick it back to you since the customer is your responsibility?

When a hard-working salesman is turned down three or four times by the same buyer, it is natural for him to brood about it. He may feel the man bears a grudge against him. He may even think there is something funny going on between the buyer and the salesman's competitors.

There Is No Conspiracy

Chances are these conjectures are wrong. The truth, in most cases, is that the purchasing agent is just doing his job. He has big responsibilities and is under constant pressure from management. If he doesn't buy a product there is a good reason that is tied up with dollars and cents rather than personal like or dislike. The salesman who probes for the reason will do more for his cause than the one who sulks and broods.

One man who learned this was Al Montrose, who sold communication equipment to electronic firms. Al had a sensitive nature and a very low boiling point. One day he flew off the handle with the purchasing agent of a big west coast firm, who had turned him down for the fifth time in a row.

"I'm going to your boss," Al thundered. "You are discriminating against me and my company, and I intend to find out why."

The purchasing agent, a veteran of 17 years on the job, remained calm.

"We'll go to him together," he replied. "I'll present your complaint to him myself in your presence."

They went to the merchandising manager who listened patiently to the whole story. Then he said to Al:

"Mr. Montrose, we don't buy items because we like some salesmen and dislike others. Nor is the reputation of the seller's company always a factor. The products we buy must meet certain specifications, most of which are set by the government. Besides, Mr. Finch (the purchasing agent) is under strict orders not to allow personal considerations to influence his decisions.

"Your products, although of top quality, simply don't meet our needs and specifications. That's the answer to your complaint."

Al matured during that meeting. He began to see buyers in a different light, not as enemies to be fought, but as conscientious men fulfilling an obligation to their company and their customers.

This is the kind of insight that more salesmen should have. Most companies feel that maintaining good relations with salesmen is good business.

"Our vendors are as important to us as we are to them," the head of a large tool company told me.

"I have given orders that salesmen are to be treated courteously and respectfully," he added.

This sums up the attitude of most firms toward salesmen. Despite what some of the disgruntled may think, there is no organized plot against sellers.

Check the Company's Buying Policy

The salesman must realize, however, that no buyer can be expected to put his time indiscriminately at the disposal of all callers. Some products or services may not be appropriate to the needs of the company, nor timely when the salesman calls. A salesman who is informed of this should be grateful. It means he doesn't have to waste time in a fruitless interview when he could be plowing more fertile soil.

One of the salesman's first jobs should be to find out the buying policies of a company.

It is a good idea to know where the firm stands and where he stands. Selling is easier if the salesman knows the ground rules. Some purchasing agents, for example, will arrange interviews between the salesman and technical, engineering or other company people if requested, or when the buyer has a doubt about the article. This is going over the buyer's head with his full knowledge and consent. It's better to do it this way than to sneak in the back door to see his boss.

Company policy embraces other selling factors. Many outfits will not disclose prices, terms and conditions submitted by competitors. There is no point in quarreling with a buyer over this matter since it is out of his hands.

Also, most companies have strict regulations governing conflict of interest. A salesman may be turned away because an employee of the firm has an interest in the supplier firm.

Knowing these policies helps eliminate conflict or ill will between salesman and buyer. When a man has had a hard day it's easy to imagine the worst—that the purchaser hates you personally or that he has a *sub rosa* deal with your competitor. These suspicions are usually groundless. The seller can make a fool of himself by running to management and crying "foul."

If he can't prove the charge (and he usually can't) he risks being *personna non grata* with that company and, perhaps, his own. It doesn't take long for word to get back to the man's supervisor that he made a fool of himself. No firm wants to keep a salesman who raises a storm every time he fails to get an order.

Remember the Purchasing Agent's Position

Remember this: The consumer can afford the luxury of buying on impulse or emotion, but the purchasing agent is not like a housewife strolling along a supermarket aisle, picking out what pleases her eye. He buys with one thought in mind: "Do we need the product?" A wrong decision can cost him his job and he knows it.

In the industrial market the agent buys on the basis of actual or expected demand by his company's customers. If the buyer firm is not moving goods, all the persuasion in the world won't help the salesman get the order. The motivations of a retail customer—vanity, prestige, fear—do not apply here.

Watch the Economy's Fluctuations

A fundamental knowledge of economics will often aid the salesman in understanding why he is not selling. The business cycle affects sales. In slack periods, companies hang tight and put off many purchases, particularly heavy, durable items like machinery. The seller must take this into account.

Don't Forget the Personal Element

There is also a personal factor involved. Some salesmen have never learned the art of human relations. They are so self-centered that they never understand why prospects and customers are cool or indifferent to them. This type of salesman has never shown the slightest interest in the buyer. He moves from office to office like a well-oiled machine, never dropping a personal comment. He forgets that buyers are human beings and like to be treated as such.

Numerous surveys have shown that prospects and customers buy from salesmen whom they believe are interested in them. A man who inquires about the prospect's health, his family, or hobby, is racking up points for himself.

Some years ago after we moved from one neighborhood to another, I went blocks out of my way to give my dry cleaning to the shop on our old street. Why? Because I felt the owner really took an interest in me and seemed to enjoy turning out first-rate work.

Often, listening carefully to a prospect, a salesman can help the man by getting him something he wants or needs for himself or his company. Such thoughtfulness will not go unrewarded. The prospect is more likely to listen more attentively to your sales talk.

One big producer, Len Mitchell, learned the birth dates of his customers' children and remembered to send or take them a little gift. Thoughtful actions like that make a deep impression on buyers.

Another way to impress prospects and customers is to offer suggestions and aids that will increase their business. This shows the buyer that you aren't merely passing through town, but that you are sincerely interested in his welfare and desire to maintain a warm relationship. His appreciation is likely to be translated into an order.

Always Avoid Friction with the Buyer

The buyer-seller relationship should be free of any prolonged friction. Of course, the two will not always get along. Both are bound to have bad days. The prospect may have been bawled out by his boss; the salesman might be suffering from indigestion or fatigue. Such conditions produce irritation, but the salesman should think twice about blowing his top. It's better to walk out and cool off than to start an argument he will regret later.

It is usually when the salesman is angry that he thinks of going over the buyer's head. If he pauses a moment he will realize that there are few problems that rational people cannot work out.

Matt Porter, salesman for a paint products firm, once found a prospect in a towering rage. He not only refused to listen to Matt's presentation, but curtly dismissed him as well. Before leaving, the salesman asked the receptionist what her boss' trouble was.

"His insurance company said it wouldn't pay a damage claim on his car, and he's been upset all day," she told Matt.

The next time Matt called on the man he recommended his own insurance broker in case he might be shopping around for a new policy. It turned out the buyer was. He was grateful for Matt's suggestion, and he apologized for his behavior the last time. That day he gave Matt a substantial order.

Without knowing the cause of the prospect's bad mood, Matt might have gone over his head to complain about his treatment. Fortunately, he was an experienced salesman and took these things in stride.

Leaping over the head of the buyer is not the ultimate solution no matter how tempted the salesman might be. It is far better to get at the root of the problem and resolve it at the lower level.

The trip upstairs may be a short one, but the long range effects can be disastrous.

15

Underrating Sales Training

MANY SALESMEN REGARD SALES TRAINING AS A CHORE TO be endured for two or three weeks and then forgotten. Some even neglect to apply the learning in the field.

This is a serious mistake. Sales training should be a continuous process, not a short-term, "shot-in-the-arm" program. The graduate of a two-week course is far from being an accomplished seller. In fact, he is just beginning to learn. A few weeks in the territory usually makes this clear.

It Is a Big Investment

Companies have invested a lot of time, money, and personnel in the training program. The firms have a genuine belief in the value of the sales courses or they wouldn't bother with them. The alert man can absorb superior product knowledge and selling skills developed and taught by experts.

But this is not enough. Salesmen should return for refresher courses to keep abreast of new products and techniques. These reviews also enable the man to acquire specific knowledge he can apply to his prospects and customers.

In other professions continuing education is taken for granted. Doctors, lawyers, engineers and accountants constantly take time out for additional learning.

Many firms consider sales training more meaningful if the men have been exposed to the field. Classes are also more interesting if the individual has encountered real problems with customers so he can benefit from the knowledge he picks up from experts. For this reason, some companies first have the trainee get out and sell and then bring him back for schooling.

Many larger firms make sure that training continues for the man after they have discharged their initial obligation. Usually this is in the hands of district managers, who are responsible for evaluating the salesman and keeping tabs on his performance.

The ambitious salesman, however, should not wait for prompting by his supervisor. He should eagerly seek out refresher courses which can give him new motivation and focus attention on bad habits that need eradication if he is to grow and prosper.

Refresher Courses Keep You Progressing

A refresher course in sales training is a kind of tonic all salesmen should take at regular intervals. Even experienced men reach a plateau after a few years on the job. On the surface all seems calm and in good order. Their work habits and attitudes are exemplary; they continue to prospect diligently for new business, and they have no emotional or personality problems. But nevertheless they know and their bosses know that they have leveled off and are no longer climbing. The bright promise they gave has faded.

If a man finds himself in this position he should not wait until his manager calls it to his attention. He should take some kind of action to get back in orbit. Volunteering for re-training could be the answer. It could give him a fresh perspective and sharpen his approach. It has worked out this way for many sales-men who have been in the doldrums.

Joe Harkness, a steel fabricator salesman, was one of those who didn't wait for the leveling off process to set in. Joe had been in the field only six months before he realized that he wasn't a ball of fire. His earnings were fair, but nothing to excite management. He had passed through his company's two-week sales training course shortly after he was hired out of college. He was then sent to a territory.

His field experience made him painfully aware of certain shortcomings. And what was worse, he could not seem to relate his training with actual prospecting and selling.

Joe made a decision. He asked permission to take the course again with a new batch of recruits. It was a wise move. The second time around really opened Joe's eyes to a lot of things he hadn't seen before.

During the re-training he realized that he had learned by rote the first time without really thinking of the application of the information his instructors threw at him. Now, with the benefit of his field work, he was able to fit the knowledge into real life experiences with customers and prospects.

The sales training course included a discussion and review of products by research, production and marketing experts in the company. In his second course, Joe was able to evaluate this important information in terms of sales—not lecture notes to be filed away and forgotten. Knowledge in selling is meaning-less if not applied. Now he could clearly see the application.

Joe became so enthusiastic about the refresher course that he took it three times. He then suggested to management an advanced course for men with three or more years in the field. The idea was adopted and proved an outstanding success.

A few years later, Joe was put in charge of the advanced course and eventually he was named head of the company's national sales training program.

This story points up the fact that a salesman cannot afford to stop learning. His future and his family's welfare depend on his growth in his organization. No man should be embarrassed or ashamed to seek outside help. Selling is rather deceptive. A big order will send a man up in the clouds. He will conveniently forget all the mediocre days and feel he is on the road marked SUCCESS. The salesman, however, must consider his continual performance—the day in and day out record. If it's run-of-the-mill, he should ask himself why. Perhaps a refresher course is what he needs.

Take Advantage of the Knowledge of the Experts

Training schools offer the latest in selling aids and product information. Instructors, drawn from all segments of the company, are experts in their respective areas. They can imbue the salesman with fresh ideas and techniques. The experience can be like a breath of cold air blowing through a foggy brain. The salesman will emerge from the course with a better understanding of his product, his competitors and the selling gam .

And if the refresher course does nothing else, it will rid the salesman of the complacency that may be afflicting him. Complacency is dangerous; from there it's only a short step to stagnation.

Sales courses also offer valuable help in presentation and human relations, both of which are important to the salesman's profits. Most sales schools are set up so that the trainee engages in real life situations in which instructors or students take the part of tough prospects or customers. The sales manager of a national food company told me:

"In our sales training program, the instructor who acts out the part of a customer is tougher, smarter and meaner than any customer the neophyte will ever face. We figure that if the trainee sells to our man he can sell to anyone."

The main reason sales training approximates reality is that the teachers have been around the track themselves. They're veterans of a thousand battles and can predict accurately what situations the salesman will encounter. They've been in the same spot themselves many, many times.

Sales Training Advice Is Sound and Up to Date

Walt Finney, a top producer for a data processing firm, once revealed to me how he became a true believer in sales training.

"I was just out of college with a major in business administration," he recalled. "I had taken two semesters of salesmanship and I felt there wasn't much the company could teach me that I couldn't learn better in the field. How wrong I was."

Walt spent six months under a district manager in California and then was sent to his firm's sales training school in Chicago.

"I realized how naive I had been," he said. "I thought I knew the ropes but they taught me some things I had never believed possible. For example, they told us we should average 30 calls a week and then showed us how to do it. It made sense.

"The instructors also gave us sound advice on getting more business from regular customers—how to stimulate consumer buying and so forth. I could see that plenty of experience had gone into their teaching. I could imagine easily how the techniques could work in my territory."

They did work. When Walt got back to his district he was a changed man. His volume took a sharp rise and kept going up. The information he brought back had a practical application with all of his prospects and customers.

Another salesman I know, Gary Cole, found the training course a mine of valuable information on streamlining his paper work.

Said Gary: "I knew they told us about paper work in the first course I took but somehow it didn't register. It was only when I started selling that I realized that bookkeeping and records were swallowing up a lot of my selling time.

"By taking the refresher course I was able to cut my homework in half. After being on the road, I could see how the instruction applied."

The point in all this is that education is a continuing process. The man who feels he has learned everything is ready for retirement. He certainly will not improve his status or income with that attitude.

And education should not stop with training programs or even refresher courses. The salesman who wants to get ahead should take every opportunity to improve himself by reading company directives, studying trade papers and industry reports and soaking up information in books, pamphlets and magazines on selling.

In our business you can never learn enough. Selling is a dynamic, rapidly changing field which demands men who can keep pace.

16

Rushing the Big Order

THE BIG TICKET CAN BE A JOYOUS REALITY OR AN ELUSIVE dream that leads the salesman to frustration and despair.

For Don Triplett, the pursuit of the big ticket ended in a nightmare of blasted hopes and bitterness. A half-million dollar contract blew up in his face after he had sweated for months to get it. It was a tough break but Don asked for it. He pushed too hard and too often, and not in the right direction. A normally bright guy, he panicked at a time he should have played it smart and cool.

A fabricated steel salesman, Don scored heavily on the first contact and followed with a solid proposal that lifted the prospect's interest pitch to a high level. But then our luckless friend stopped selling and started pestering.

Day after day he was on the buyer's back, a fountain pen clutched in his hot hand. He hounded the man for a decision so often that finally the latter couldn't stand it anymore. The prospect eventually refused to accept Don's phone calls or receive him in the office, except once—the day he called off the deal.

There is no happy ending to the story. Don lost the order

period. He made the tragic mistake of not building on his initial presentation until the contract was in his pocket.

Instead of pressing his advantage with creative salesmanship, Don was sailing on Cloud 9, dreaming of the Florida vacation and the new home his commission would buy.

The bad news caught him completely unprepared. He had thought the contract was in the bag, and needed only a slight nudge or two.

The Incubation Period

A big order undergoes an incubation period. There's often a long silence between the early favorable response and the actual signing. The purchasing agent is only the first step. The final decision rests with various company officers up to and including the president. Even the stockholders may be consulted. These men are not going to be pressured into an approval by constant nuisance calls from the salesman. After all, a half-million dollar deal is not the same as buying a new typewriter.

A big ticket order must simmer. Turn up the flame too high and you burn yourself out of a commission.

Take Constructive Action

But there is plenty of *constructive* action the salesman can take to swing the decision in his favor. After arousing the prospect's interest, he must *keep* it. This means understanding the buyer's special problems and offering solutions and applications that convince him the salesman has a genuine interest in helping him.

The salesman with the big ticket on the fire must make sure his follow-up calls are meaningful, not repetitious and time-wasting. Can the salesman come up with a sound idea for cutting the prospect's production costs by $2,000 a month? Has he analyzed all the customer's objections and prepared effective answers? Does he work on new demonstrations and other techniques that nail down his case at the strategic time?

These are some of the *positive* moves a salesman can make to write up the big ticket. The seller who thinks only of himself, his commission, his interest, will suffer Don Triplett's fate. Purchasers have an uncanny sense of smelling out pure selfishness. They know when the salesman is merely plugging himself and when he is offering constructive assistance.

Many salesmen are baffled by the long hiatus between the initial presentation and the close. They know they have done a good job in warming up the prospect. They touched all bases at the first or second meeting. The demonstrations were adroitly handled. Why then the delay?

Handling Home Office Pressure

The suspense is even more grueling when there is pressure on the salesman from his home office to which the order could mean the difference between profit and loss for the year. In this situation both the salesman and headquarters are usually unaware of the below surface activity in the prospect firm. Perhaps a merger or acquisition is planned. A managerial shakeup may be in the works or a current tax tangle is causing concern. The decision to buy could be hung up on any one of these factors.

A friend of mine, Dave Lansing, once lost 15 pounds from worry and loss of sleep while anxiously waiting to close a $300,000 order from a drug chain. Every time he thought he had the deal wrapped up, he hit another stall. This continued for six months.

He was about to kiss the whole thing off when the prospect called him one day.

"We're ready to sign," the executive announced.

Dave hurried over and the formalities were cleaned up in 15 minutes.

The prospect said he was sorry about the delay and explained that his firm just bought out a west coast outfit which would double its size.

"We couldn't move on the order until we completed the merger," the official told Dave.

Seek the Cause of the Delay

In this instance the company had clamped such tight security around its negotiations that Dave had no idea what was up. Often, however, an alert salesman can ferret out the reason for the procrastination and switch his offense to meet it.

Sources he can tap include the Dun & Bradstreet reports, the firm's own annual report, people in the industry, trade magazines, and the prospect company's personnel, supervisors, secretaries, junior executives, etc. Rumors fly fast in a business organization and it isn't long before even the janitors know something is in the wind.

And don't forget that the competition isn't sleeping while you're mooning over the big order. The salesman's toughest hurdle to the close may be a rival proposal. The prospect will naturally make the best deal for his company that he can. The objective then is to learn the competitor's proposition and try to top it in cost, quality, service, reputation or anything else you can drag out from your arsenal. Keep fighting back—counterpunch hard and fast.

The late Thomas J. Watson of IBM once gave this advice to salesmen:

"Keep track of those people who say 'no' because next week, next month or next year they are going to say 'yes' to somebody who is selling your kind of product. Selling is a building proposition."

Mr. Watson's warning should be heeded by the salesman who smugly assumes the momentum from his initial presentation will carry him all the way to victory.

The importance of the follow-through crops up in many other lines of endeavor.

A successful lawyer, no matter how strong his case, will never take a jury for granted. He'll keep hammering away until the final moment of the trial. Or take politics. On a November night in 1948, Thomas E. Dewey went to bed with the comfortable assurance that he would be the president of the United States the next morning. But a man named Harry Truman and his advisers weren't especially impressed by the pollsters and other "experts" who predicted a landslide victory for Dewey. Truman continued to campaign right up to the wire.

You all know the result of that election.

Perseverance also marked the career of Thomas A. Edison. Most people know that Edison was a great inventor, but he also was a powerhouse salesman who obtained capital for his projects by presenting compelling arguments to hard-headed investors.

Edison's motto was: "There is no substitute for hard work."

That should also be the salesman's credo. Wishful thinking, trusting to luck, or past successes will not snare the order. Only constant, directed effort will put the salesman in the big ticket class.

And don't give up even though it might seem as if you're just treading water and not getting anywhere.

Whenever I run into a discouraged salesman chasing an important contract, I tell him about the old Third Avenue El in New York.

I used to lunch with friends at a seafood restaurant near the structure. From the window we would watch the demolition. Hundreds of workmen nibbled away at the gigantic steel pillars with acetylene torches and sledge hammers.

But despite all the burning and battering, the old edifice

seemed destined to remain upright forever, a mighty and impossible challenge to the puny men below. We began to bet on
how long the El would survive the onslaught.

Then one day it was all over. A single hammer blow and the
massive beams crashed down with a thundering roar.

The demolition gang knew it would happen that way; that
each moment brought them closer to their objective, regardless of how impregnable the El looked to bystanders.

Build a Strong Foundation

So it is with selling. You must keep swinging at the prospect,
renewing the battle again and again. But don't return to nag,
plead or whine. Show up with fresh ideas and new approaches
that will break down his resistance.

The prospect welcomes a constructive review of his problems. Give him ammunition he can take to his superiors. If a
purchasing agent tells you the proposition must be submitted
to a "buying committee," give him enough facts and material
to do a selling job for you. Most important, make sure the agent
is sold on you and the project before he goes to the committee.
It may be your biggest and last chance to grab the big ticket.

If you're stuck for a fresh angle, sell the prospect on your
organization. Let him know that your outfit is going all out for
research and development, new production methods, promotion and expansion. The large order demands a lot of follow-up
work by you and your company. The buyer will sleep better if
he knows that his account will be expertly serviced and backed
by generous advertising and promotion. A firm dealing out a
six-figure order doesn't want to get involved with a fly-by-night
or weak supplier.

Never beg for the order on the basis of personal need or
gratification. Business firms aren't charity foundations and your
troubles are not their concern.

The vice president of a large west coast plastics manufacturer told me of a salesman who lost a $200,000 order because he used the wrong technique.

"The guy made a sound initial presentation," the executive said, "but he did nothing to impress us after that.

"We couldn't give him a quick decision and he began making a pest of himself to everyone from the receptionist to the president. We put up with it because we had enjoyed good relations with his firm. But then he pulled a real boner.

"It seems his company was running some kind of contest for salesmen with a big bonus for the man who met a certain quota. This fellow said he had to have our order to push him over the top. Well, right away we could see he was not at all concerned with our problems, but only with his own glory. We said good-bye to him for the last time."

Any salesman has the right to think of his own future and security, but selling is a two-way street. If you give something, you'll get something in return. Show the prospect you're conscientiously trying to help him and he'll be grateful.

A salesman pursuing the big ticket will often find the situation stalled on dead center. This is the time to shower the prospect with live, workable, money-saving ideas. Then, the big ticket will write itself.

17

Being an Ungracious Host

MOST SALESMEN KNOW HOW TO TAKE ADVANTAGE OF A break when it comes their way. A sad exception is the trade show.

Here is a made-to-order situation for the seller. All he has to do is stand at a booth and the prospect *comes to him*—no cooling heels in reception rooms, no fighting for a busy buyer's time.

You would think the salesman would jump at the opportunity of a trade show. After all, half the battle is won merely by being a gracious host.

But it doesn't work that way.

For the past several years I have attended at least one trade show a week at the Coliseum and at numerous hotels in New York and around the country. I've taken a close look at how salesmen operate at these functions. I'm not impressed.

The Something-for-Nothing Attitude

The trouble is that these men have too much of a good thing. They think they merely have to stand there with a stock smile and a badge and they have it made. They expect the prospect to beat a path to their booth, pen in hand. How wrong can they be?

Most of the salesmen I saw were failing in common courtesy. Instead of showing a genuine interest in the buyer's needs, the salesman took the "me" attitude. He wanted to shoot out a quick glad hand and write up an order.

This salesman certainly wouldn't act that way as a host in his own home. Yet, here he is playing host at a trade show and performing like a boor.

I have met many salesmen at these shows. Some were a credit to their business, but the majority gave their profession and their employers a black eye. Many times I waited vainly for a "host" salesman to ask me what he could do for me. Instead, he was more interested in finding out who I was and where I was from. It gave me the feeling that he was trying to decide if I were important enough to merit his time. Seldom did a salesman have the good grace to thank me for stopping at his booth.

I remember one man shaking my hand while he was looking over my shoulder at somebody else he thought more important. I wondered later how many people he had brushed off that way during the show.

You Are Dealing with Busy Men

This sort of conduct is bad public relations for the selling field. These buyers are busy men. They attend trade shows to buy, get information or plan for the future. And they're doing it at their own expense.

If I were to point out anyone as a fine example of a trade show host, it would be Bill Hawkins.

Bill began his career as an actor. He didn't have much success on the stage, appearing only in minor roles. Eventually, he went into selling and really found his true vocation. The poise and manners he had learned as an actor were put to good use at trade shows. Bill made such a pleasing impression at these functions that his company, which runs ten shows a year, appointed him to direct them. He also trains other salesmen how to act at the shows.

Here is another thought on the subject. One of the major league baseball parks has a corps of ushers who are world famous for their gracious, courteous treatment of patrons. These men are so outstanding in their jobs that they are in constant demand for other events between seasons. Now, if these ushers, who are performing a rather menial task, can operate this way, surely a salesman, with much more at stake, can do likewise. The ushers are only playing host for a $2.50 or $3.50 ticket holder. You, as a sales person, may be jeopardizing a six-figure contract by behaving badly at a trade show.

He Also Serves . . .

The salesman has a responsibility to be a gracious host. He should welcome the opportunity to demonstrate what he can do for the customer. He should also be grateful that the buyer singled him out. Here is Mohammed coming to the mountain. Learn how to take advantage of it.

Here is some trade show advice for salesmen:

1. Before the show, write a personal letter to every prospect in the community, telling him you're looking forward to seeing him.
2. When the prospect shows up, thank him sincerely for *giving you his time.*
3. Impress upon him that you consider this a wonderful opportunity to let him tell you what *you can do for him.*
4. Be prepared to discuss *his* problems with understanding and intelligence.
5. Following the show, write another letter to your visi-

tors, thanking them for stopping by. (Do this whether you got an order or not.)

6. At the same time, let him know you will call on him soon "to pick up where we left off."

7. If a major account representative has visited your booth, suggest that your president contact the man and thank him for his interest.

8. Don't mix work and play. If you are assigned a booth, stay put. A buyer who is giving you a portion of his precious time should not be forced to look for you in the "Hospitality Suite." Of course, there is a time for socializing, but don't think of the trade show as an extended party. Your customer may have to get back to his office.

More ideas to improve trade show selling will occur to the man with a good sense of public relations. Put your best foot forward at these affairs.

Remember, a trade show isn't a college or Army reunion. These functions vitally affect your livelihood, your employer and your future. The trade show visitors are the people you hope will buy your product. If they go away with a poor impression of you, what chance do you think you have for selling them in the future?

Big Accounts Can Be Lost or Won

The right attitude and deportment can lead to years of profitable association with customers. Ignorance of proper behavior may ruin your effectiveness as a salesman.

A few years ago a young man, Ed Miller, was given an important assignment at a west coast show for the paper carton industry. A mild-looking, somewhat quiet person stopped at Ed's booth and asked a few questions. The fellow did not strike Ed as anyone of consequence and he treated him brusquely, even rudely. He did not even bother to get the man's name or company.

Ed's boss appeared a few minutes later, hopping mad.

"It might interest you to know," he snapped, "that the little guy you so lightly dismissed happens to be a top manager of one of the nation's biggest dairies. They spend millions for dairy product cartons."

Ed wasn't fired. His boss gave him a break because of his youth and inexperience. Besides, the boss figures that the young man had learned his lesson. He had.

There is a lesson here for all salesmen. A little time spent in being courteous at a trade show is simply good business practice. It's also part of your job.

18

Not Handling the Product with Care

WHILE DINING IN A FINE RESTAURANT ONE EVENING, I noticed the proud, almost loving way in which our waiter presented the food. Each dish was set down with a flourish. We were made to feel that we were fortunate indeed to be permitted to spend our money there. That restaurant had learned the art of presentation. Its food, although good, was not extraordinary. But each diner was made to feel like a king eating off gold plates.

Showing Will Not Do the Complete Job

There is an important lesson here for salesmen. One of the basic mistakes in selling is the smug assurance that the mere showing of the product and the explaining of its features are enough.

The salesman who handles his products in a casual, offhand way is inviting an indifferent reception from the prospect. But let the buyer see that you hold the item with tender care and his interest will be lifted.

Look at it this way: If the product could sell itself without the salesman's presence, why not simply send a sample to the prospect and let it go at that? The answer is obvious. The personal touch is as necessary to selling as water is to plants.

The salesman should handle his product like a rare diamond. His voice, attitude and gestures should convey absolute respect and admiration for the line. A master at the art of presentation can make even a shoddy piece of goods take on a new aura: think what you can do with a good product.

The vice president of a company which had consulted me was worried about inroads the competition was making into his market.

"I can't understand it," he told me. "We're doing as much advertising and promotion as they are and yet we can't catch up."

I investigated the matter thoroughly and came to this conclusion: The firm's salesmen were giving little or no attention to the finer points of presentation. They were content to merely show the product, explain its features and then depend on providence to see them through. It was a mechanical procedure as automatic as packing and unpacking a suitcase. I didn't know what the opposition was doing but it could not have been any worse.

For the next two weeks I buttonholed every salesman in the firm. I urged them to study everything that was presented to them in their daily lives—food, clothing, shoes, automobiles, advertisements, etc.

"Observe," I said, "how the seller handles the product."

I accompanied one salesman to a shoe store where the clerk caressed the tip of the shoes while presenting them.

"That man makes considerably less than you do, but look at the love he puts into his work," I remarked to the salesman.

At a jewelry store, the clerk delicately placed a half-dozen watches on a black velvet cloth for our inspection. The gesture reeked of quality.

"If you don't think highly of your product," I told the salesman, "how do you expect the prospect to give it value?"

The advice took hold. Within six months sales shot up in every territory. Good salesmen became better salesmen and I heard no more about the competition.

The salesman should also create an atmosphere of quality by the clothes he wears and the cases he carries. I know a sales manager who bought each of his men gold Swiss watches of the finest quality. The watches never failed to excite the prospect's interest. They gave the men an air of confidence, well-being and above all—quality.

The prospect may not mention your expensive new tie or suit, but he will note it and evaluate you and your product accordingly.

A Salesman Is Something of an Actor

I have always felt that acting and salesmanship are close cousins. The salesman can learn a great deal from an actor or actress. They play their roles convincingly night after night for a year or longer. It matters not that they have recited the lines hundreds of times. Each night is a new performance with a new audience.

The audience expects a fresh, lively performance and usually gets it. The salesman must also remember that each prospect is a new audience who has the right to his best performance, for when a salesman is presenting goods he is putting on a performance. He doesn't have to resort to histrionics, but all the same the prospect is watching to see how he conducts himself.

A buyer will react to a salesman's presentation just as he would to an actor's performance. If the seller is dull, apathetic and disinterested, the prospect will find a means of terminating the interview. On the other hand, a bright, sharp presentation will tune up the prospect like a violin.

Many sales are lost because the salesman left his enthusiasm at home. He handled his product as if it were a dollar watch.

There are two basic parts to the making of a sale:

1. The product and its features.
2. The man making the presentation.

The second is equally as important as the first.

Getting the customer's attention, arousing his interest, creating desire and closing the sale—all these depend on the strength of the presentation. To translate an abstract idea into concrete reality for the prospect requires good presentation. Presentation is the means whereby the salesman can demonstrate that his product is superior and worth buying.

In a retail store an alert salesman will handle even a necktie with loving care. Can the territorial salesman do any less if he is to survive?

The answer should be obvious.

19

Depending on One Answer to an Objection

FLEXIBILITY IS THE MARK OF A GOOD SALESMAN.

In the hurly-burly of business, we often lose sight of the fact that salesmanship is a creative, dynamic force, calling for imaginative, well-trained personnel. The salesman who can't shift position and tactics to meet new situations, will always run out of the money. This is particularly true of the man who can't handle objections.

A king-sized mistake is preparing only one answer to an objection or argument thrown by the prospect. Many salesmen memorize their one reply and go off confidently on their calls. If the buyer is dissatisfied with the pat reply, the salesman can only stammer and flush with embarrassment.

Inflexibility Is Insufficient Preparation

Military commanders always have an alternate plan if the first maneuver fails, or for some reason is unworkable. A quarterback will always have another pass target if the main receiver can't break free. These men know the danger in a rigid pattern of behavior.

Disaster also lurks for the salesman who dumps all his hopes on one answer to an objection, *regardless of how thoroughly he knows that answer.*

My friend, Dale Mickelson, was just such a salesman. He had a neat, compartmentalized mind that functioned on a single track. He shrewdly anticipated objections to his presentation and produced an answer for each one.

The roof fell in one day while he was interviewing a tough prospect.

Dale, who sold planing mill machinery, delivered a scintillating sales talk and then it was the buyer's move. He tossed out three or four objections that Dale fielded neatly. All the answers had satisfied previous customers.

But this character was far from satisfied. He informed Dale that all his proposed solutions had been tried in the plant and failed. This left the salesman nowhere to go but out. A big order went down the drain.

Take a Lesson from a Lawyer

That night, Dale and his wife were invited to the home of his brother, a prominent tort lawyer. My friend, still feeling bruised from his clobbering, unloaded his burden on his host.

"Well," his brother injected, "I don't know much about selling, but it appears to me that you were unprepared. I'd get murdered in a courtroom if I tried to stand on a case as weak as yours."

"What do you mean?" Dale asked.

The lawyer explained that pre-trial preparation involved painstaking research for precedents that will support an attorney's case.

"We don't stop at one citation," he went on. "We find as many as we can to present to the court. A judge often makes his decision on the basis of such arguments. The other side in the trial is doing the same thing and victory or defeat can hang on the question of who can bring in the most effective citations."

Furthermore, the lawyer said, an attorney had to be prepared to meet objections from opposing counsel.

Dale was so intrigued that he attended four or five trials the following weeks. He was amazed at the amount of information lawyers furnished the judges in support of their cases. In time, he was able to distinguish between lawyers who had built solid cases and those who tried to get by on flamboyance and oratory.

The courtroom time wasn't wasted. Dale learned a great deal about the value of preparation. He put his knowledge into practice by compiling a list of every possible objection he could expect from prospects. Beneath each one he wrote from 10 to 15 answers and counterarguments.

To obtain the data, he made a complete restudy of his product line, seeking facts from his sales manager, the engineers, production experts and marketing specialists in his company. Then he memorized the information until he could recite it verbatim. But, at the same time, he taught himself to shift field if warranted by a prospect's particular line of questioning. He learned to be flexible.

It's a Great Feeling to Be Prepared

There was a delightful bonus in this for Dale. Instead of being nervous and tense when objections were hurled at him, he found himself actually enjoying the exchange with the buyer. He looked forward to it, in fact. The give and take afforded him an opportunity to demonstrate his secure knowledge of the product and his firm. He felt at ease—sure of himself. On occasion, he would even encourage the prospect to speak his mind.

An experienced salesman fears the silent prospect more than

the guy who breaks in with frequent objections. If a buyer listens without ever commenting, it could mean that he is apathetic to the presentation and is only waiting for a lull to terminate the interview. Objections, on the other hand, tip off the salesman to the prospect's thinking and tell him how much progress he has made. When I was selling I worried only when the prospect sat there without saying a word. If he tried to tear holes in my proposition, I felt the interview was running my way.

But to get back to Dale Mickelson—he became so adept at blocking objections that his volume soared within a few months. Now and then a prospect would stump him, but very rarely. When this occurred, Dale was honest enough to admit he did not have the answer and promised to check it out immediately. The next day he was in the buyer's office with the relevant facts. He found that this policy paid off in the confidence and reliance the prospect placed in him.

If You Don't Know, Don't Argue

One thing Dale did *not* do was argue with the prospect. A salesman loses points when he turns an interview into a debate. There are times when the buyer is wrong and the salesman knows it. However, it's bad psychology to throw the mistake into the man's face. So much more can be accomplished by diplomacy—being pleasant and understanding. Bluntness may satisfy the salesman's ego, but it will do nothing to garner an order. Besides, it is bad manners.

There are many artful ways to let the prospect know that his argument lacks merit. Raising his temper certainly won't bring him to your side.

Every salesman should be a student of human nature. Prospects are people. They have their vanity and pride as does everyone else. Don't ruin a sale because you insist on being right all the time. Give him the benefit of the doubt and then release your big guns on his argument. The really clever salesman gives the prospect the impression that he's agreeing with his objections and then skillfully shows him they are unfounded. I am not recommending deception. Above all, play it straight if you want to survive in selling. But, if you can score a touchdown by going around end more easily, why plunge through the middle?

Jack Bryant, a plywood salesman, developed this technique to such a fine art that the prospect would usually forget all about his objections at the end of the interview. Jack operated on a very simple philosophy: he knew more about his product than the buyer. He utilized this knowledge to steer the interview in his direction.

As Jack explained to me: "If a prospect takes over the interview, I'm finished. That's why I maintain a list of twenty answers to any objection I might encounter.

"The buyer, of course, knows his own problems and needs, but often I find that he's been misinformed about my line. Most objections are the result of misinformation that must be corrected."

20

Ignoring Aid from Your Supervisors

MANY FIRMS ASSIGN A SUPERVISOR TO ACCOMPANY A NEW salesman around his territory to show him the ropes.

Some companies also will delegate a sales manager to travel with a man whose volume has been falling off. In this case, the supervisor acts as a kind of morale builder.

Do Not Judge or Expect Miracles

In either instance it's a mistake for the salesman to pass judgment on his superior or to expect some kind of miracle performance. Yet this is exactly what happens all too often. Instead of learning from the supervisor, the salesman takes a sharply critical attitude.

He may comment to his colleagues or his wife: "Joe Smith, the district manager, was with me for a week and what a bust he was. He didn't pick up one order. How does he expect me to come through?"

This salesman misses the whole point of having the manager along. The supervisor does not have to prove himself to him or anyone else. He already has demonstrated his ability to the company's satisfaction. His position is proof of that.

The manager is simply acting as a guide to give the man the benefit of his experience and knowledge of the product, company and customers.

The supervisor is definitely not trying to show the salesman up by getting orders. This would be bad human relations and the company recognizes that fact.

In fact, some firms make it a practice to have one of its sales supervisors accompany the men periodically in their territory. This is a form of customer relations that often pays big dividends in terms of sales.

A good example of this was John Malcom, who sold food ingredients to canners and food processors in the Middle West.

There was a morale problem in the sales force of John's company. Many of the men resented the company's policy of sending out supervisors with them. He overheard bitter remarks from salesmen about supervisors "butting in" on interviews.

One day another salesman told John: "One of the bosses went with me last week and didn't do a nickel's worth of business. As far as I was concerned, he was just extra baggage to take along."

John, however, was producing very well and the company saw no need to give him any supervisorial assistance.

Nevertheless, John thought there was something wrong in the attitude of the salesmen. Surely, he reasoned, the sales managers have knowledge and techniques that could benefit a man. All of them began as salesmen and worked their way up through the ranks. They should be top men.

John decided to make use of these talents. Instead of avoiding assistance, he asked the firm for one of its sales supervisors or department heads to join him on his calls each season. The company was surprised at the request but was glad to comply.

Get the Benefit of His Years of Experience

On these trips John made it a point not to judge the supervisor but to learn all he could from him. By keeping his eyes and ears open he began to be aware of weaknesses in his own presentation, technique and product knowledge. He was getting the benefit of the man's many years of experience. John had been a good salesman. He now realized he was going to be a better one. The net result of John's learning was that he went into a much higher income bracket in the next three years.

When he returned from his trips he appointed himself a committee of one to boost the idea of supervisors accompanying salesmen on calls for the first few months or when a man was in the doldrums.

He convinced several of the men that the supervisor could be a valuable asset in selling. John emphasized, however, that the salesman must be free from bitterness and regard the manager with objectivity.

"Forget your pride and your prejudices and look upon him as a friend, not an enemy," John urged the salesmen.

That was the whole key to the problem. Several of the salesmen had thought of the accompanying supervisor as some kind of spy for the company. They were fearful and suspicious and no rapport was possible. The upshot was that the two-man trips, designed for the salesman's benefit, were seldom successful. John's solid endorsement of the plan allayed the men's fears.

John became so involved in his new role that the company thought he ought to make a career of it. He was appointed a trouble shooter for low-yield territories. Periodically, he travels with a regular salesman whose volume has fallen off. John's job is to jack up the volume without bruising the man's ego or driving him to another company. This, of course, calls for tact and ability—qualities which John has in abundance. Between John and the men there is a feeling of mutual respect.

Far from being reluctant to have him, many of the salesmen and sales managers put in requests for John's services and he is always booked months in advance. In addition, the customers are glad to see him. He makes good friends for the firm.

But John's relationship with the salesmen is a two-way street. He learns from them at the same time he is giving them the benefit of his knowledge and experience. No one person possesses all sales "savvy." The rawest recruit can sometimes come up with a technique that will dazzle men who are years in advance of him in experience.

Get Constructive Criticism Immediately

One of the advantages of having two men on a sales call is that it helps the salesman analyze failures immediately after they happen. The supervisor or department head can point out where he missed an opportunity, overlooked an important factor or did not press an advantage. If the error is caught in time, the man may be able to return the next day and clinch the order.

It is often difficult for a salesman to level with himself as to his conduct during a call. All of us tend to magnify our good points and conveniently fail to acknowledge our bad ones. It's human nature. An understanding sales manager can be a big help to a man in this respect.

As an objective observer of the salesman's performance, he can tell if he was courteous, pleasant, patient, understanding, clear or tactful. It is sometimes possible for a man to commit a blunder or offend a customer without his being aware of it. Did he push too hard when a soft sell was called for? Did he rub the prospect the wrong way by mentioning a taboo subject? Usually the supervisor can spot these mistakes and suggest a remedy that will save the day. The mere smoking of a cigarette is enough to spoil a sale with some people.

One large farm machinery firm not only sends a sales man-

ager out with a new salesman, but the former also keeps score
on the fellow. This is done with the salesman's complete knowledge. At first the men were skeptical of the idea, but now give
it their unqualified endorsement. The rating sheets kept by the
supervisors have turned up some weaknesses which might never
have been discovered otherwise. They are discussed in an
atmosphere of good will and understanding. The salesman is
told that nobody expected him to bat 1,000 on his first trip out
and that the errors were expected. It was then explained that
the man's earnings would rise if the mistakes were corrected.

I met Whit Trombley, one of that company's top salesmen,
at a convention in St. Louis.

He said he owed a large part of his success to the performance
record on him kept by a supervisor during Whit's first few
months with the firm.

"My problem was one of appearance and manner although
I didn't realize it," he recalled. "I knew my sales talk cold, but
I just wasn't getting over to the buyers.

"The company assigned one of the district managers, Jack
Wilson, to make several calls with me. At the end of a week
Jack put his finger right on the heart of my mistakes. He told
me my presentation lacked conviction because I didn't look
directly at the prospect but made speeches at the window or
wall.

"The supervisor also noticed that I had a habit of jingling
change in my pocket to the annoyance of prospects and customers. When I got rid of these little drawbacks and a few
others my sales started to climb."

Whit is one of many salesmen who have had the same experience. When a man is starting out, selling can be a tough
business. It helps to have someone along who has been through
it before and can make the going a little easier.

So, don't sit in jdugment on the man showing you the ropes.
Let him be your guide and teacher.

We can learn by watching others.

21

Accepting Dismissal without a Fight

A SALESMAN'S LIFE WOULD BE A GOOD DEAL EASIER IF every prospect welcomed him with open arms. But we all know this is not the case. Many a man who gets a foot in the door only has to pull it out again because of an abrupt dismissal by the prospect.

You are all familiar with the dismissal techniques. They are really excuses rather than objections. Here are a few examples:

1. We are loyal to our present supplier from whom we have bought for 25 years.
2. Your price is too high.
3. This is inventory week. I can't buy.
4. I'll think it over.
5. My budget is all used up. See me in about six months when I have a new budget.
6. We buy your product from a brother-in-law of one of our vice presidents.
7. I'll contact you.

There are many others but this gives you an idea.

Resistance Is Often Insincere

Some of these excuses are genuine but in 90 percent of the cases they are not. The resistance by the buyer is insincere. He is concealing his true reason for not giving you an order.

He may not want to admit that he buys a lower-price line, or that he does not have the authority to make a purchase. Also, the prospect may not be sure in his own mind what he wants to do and so stalls the salesman with the first excuse that comes into his head. Then there is the buyer who feels that he must say "no" the first time as a matter of form; he thinks it's expected of him. He may also merely want to test a salesman's reaction to an indifferent or negative reception.

"That's all very well," you say, "but salesmen are not mind readers. How can we tell what lies behind the prospect's statement?"

You can't, but you don't have to let excuses discourage you either. It's a mistake not to put up a fight against this kind of buyer resistance. Don't crawl away at the first growl.

Uncover the Real Reason

The salesman should stand his ground at any cost. If he can weather the prospect's initial reaction, he can usually stay long enough to make a firm presentation.

The idea is to get behind the smoke screen the prospect is throwing up. The salesman must keep digging until he has found the *real* reason for the dismissal tactic.

Ken Forbes, a young salesman for a mill supply manufacturer, ran into just exactly this kind of situation. Before he could tell his story he found himself being invited to leave. Prospects were using the stock excuses mentioned previously.

At periodic sales meetings of this firm, Ken learned that he was not an isolated case. Many of the veteran salesmen discussed the various techniques prospects had used to shut them out. He heard of one buyer, for example, who played favorites and always offered phony excuses to salesmen not on his "preferred" list.

Some of the old timers with Ken's firm were big producers. Somehow, Ken reasoned, they must have found an effective way to overcome the dismissal device. If they could do it, he could too, he decided.

Ken began to develop an instinct about prospects who gave him a quick brush-off. He noticed that their excuse for not buying was made automatically, a conditioned reflex. When this happened Ken held his ground and then started boring in. He began asking questions such as, "Why do you have to think it over?"

Or: "Why do you think you can't afford our product?"

Whenever the prospect gave an excuse, Ken knocked it down. He was like a professional boxer, weaving and ducking until he could maneuver inside his opponent's guard for the blow that counts.

In time, Ken found there was little to the excuses in most cases. They were simply put up as dummies to conceal the real motives of the buyers. He was careful not to ridicule or make fun of the excuse, however paltry. Instead he would ask, "Is there another reason holding you back, Mr. Brown?" Or, "Is there something you haven't told me?" The first few times he tried this he was surprised by the frank and warm response. It seemed as if the prospect had been waiting for an opportunity to unburden himself.

Counter with Sales Points

Another method employed by Ken to counter hostile questions was to answer them by making sales points close to the buyer's opposition. For example, if he thought a prospect asked an unfriendly question merely as an excuse, Ken would not reply directly to the query. Such a question might be: "Aren't you having labor trouble?"

Ken would reply: "We have one of the most highly skilled labor forces in the country."

Remember that purchasing agents operate under all kinds of restrictions.

Can you imagine an agent telling a salesman "I can't buy from you because I don't have the authority to make this kind of purchase"?

Or do you think he would admit that he was powerless to act because his boss plays golf with the president of a competing company?

Of course the salesman will have to be satisfied with some excuses, valid or not. There are times when the prospect won't budge from his position. He is not his own man. There is also the fact no one company can distribute its business to every salesman who calls. If a particular industry does $100 million of business and there are 75 to 110 producers in that industry, the average manufacturer will get only from one to five percent of the total volume.

This does not mean, however, that a salesman should accept every excuse at its face value. The man who does that is not going very far in selling. If the salesman keeps hammering away at the dismissal device, sooner or later he'll hit an excuse that won't stand up under scrutiny. It may take more than one call —perhaps as many as five or six. But the effort will be worth it. Surveys show that 20 percent of salesmen make five or more calls on a prospect and close 80 percent of the business.

Many times the salesman can forearm himself against an expected excuse. By doing a little checking around in the industry he can come prepared with ammunition.

Relax the Prospective Buyer

There is another thing I've learned. There is no sense in trying to high-pressure a buyer whose guard goes up the moment a salesman approaches him. If the seller pushes too hard the prospect is lost for good. The best method is to get the man to relax by word, action or attitude. Let him know that the decision to buy or not to buy is strictly up to him. Feed him only facts and information that will help him make up his mind or change it. If the sale is not made, the effort still has not been wasted. The salesman has built up trust and confidence that will pay off for him the next time he calls.

A tricky statement from a buyer is, "I'm too busy to talk now." This could be an excuse, or the man may really be sincere. The salesman must watch himself here. The wrong response could ruin him with the prospect.

If the salesman really believes the man is busy or even if he's in doubt, he should leave his card and depart. If the man is convinced the prospect is simply using it as an excuse, the salesman should have something to say immediately. Without seeming to doubt the man's word, the salesman must quickly demonstrate to the prospect that he cannot afford NOT to give him some time.

Some Simple Rules to Heed

There is no single technique to counter excuses or bona fide objections. Each must be taken on its merits and handled as the salesman sees fit. There are a few basic rules, however, that should be followed:

1. *Don't go away mad.* Go or stay, but do it with good grace. Don't be a sorehead.
2. *Don't argue.*
3. *Be tactful.* Even if the excuse is so thin as to be laughable, don't laugh. With a straight face, handle it diplomatically.
4. *Don't try to steamroller through an excuse.* It must be countered with facts that will capture the prospect's

imagination and make him forget about dismissing you.
5. *Help the buyer make up his mind.* Give him hard facts that he can take back to his boss.

Keep in mind that many prospects, purchasing agents, etc., have trained themselves to become experts in the art of dismissal. It's second nature to them. So must the salesman become an expert in holding fast until the prospect has exhausted his arguments.

You can't win them all, but you can win enough to afford that vacation in Bermuda.

22

Running with the Pack

Henry Ford once told his production staff: "Make the cars any color you like as long as it's black."

Now, of course, Ford and other automobiles are made in all colors and most people wouldn't have it any other way. Colors, like styles, express individuality and personal taste.

Salesmen, too, should express individuality. There should be something about a man's appearance, manner or approach that makes him stand out in a prospect's mind.

Many salesmen make the mistake of being afraid to be different. They run with the pack, blend with the herd. They actually seem to seek anonymity by dressing, talking and acting like every other salesman. So indistinguishable have they become that a buyer has forgotten them two minutes after they leave his office.

The business world is smothered in so much conformity today that anyone who breaks the pattern of accepted standards is likely to succeed on the strength of his courage alone. Sometimes only a daring new idea is needed.

The advertising man who thought of putting a patch over the eye of a male shirt model won a big reputation for himself and sold a lot of shirts. A proper Englishman with a beard has performed a miraculous sales job for what was a relatively obscure tonic water. A general named George Patton captured yards of newspaper space because he wore two pearl-handled six shooters at his side.

An actress named Garbo became the most talked about woman on two continents merely because she made herself *unavailable.*

Develop a Distinguishing Characteristic

These persons all have one thing in common—a distinguishing characteristic. They stood out from the mob. They defied classification or typing.

Salesmen can learn from these examples. I don't mean that a man must swing from the chandelier or play a trumpet solo for the prospect, but he should acquire or develop some characteristic which sets him apart from the thousands of other salesmen competing for attention. This can mean a major or minor alteration in the man's habits or appearance.

One fellow I know, Dick Trainor, grew a neat Van Dyke beard because he thought he had a "common face."

At first he endured a lot of kidding from his colleagues and some customers, but in the long run the gimmick paid off. The facial adornment gradually took on a new meaning for the people who knew him. Dick was different. He could be told apart from the 200 other salesmen peddling the same product.

Dick, incidentally, sold printing ink. A study of the competing products had convinced him that only the label and the shape of the container differentiated his ink from the others. There seemed little likelihood that his product would change, so he decided to alter himself, to become a personality prospects and customers would remember. It turned out to be the best move he ever made. Prospects who previously had been cold became deferential to Dick. In time, he adopted a style to go with the beard which always was fastidiously trimmed. He began to spend less and less time in waiting rooms. It seemed that prospects sought *him* out. In two years his earnings had doubled.

All because of a beard? Not quite. Dick was a first-rate salesman. But so were many others. The beard simply helped him realize his true potential. It gave him the opportunity to really show what he could do.

Another friend of mine, Lyle Shore, acquired his distinguishing feature in an entirely accidental way.

While vacationing in Europe several years ago, he bought a suit of the finest English woolen from an exclusive London tailor. The purchase was made on sheer impulse.

When he returned home he occasionally wore the suit on his sales calls. It never failed to evoke admiring comments from prospects and customers. Everyone remarked on what excellent taste he had.

That sparked an idea. Lyle began ordering all his clothes from London—suits, shirts, shoes, neckwear and even socks. He wore clothes well and soon began to look like a fashion model for Saville Row. His apparel, the best obtainable, became a conversation piece wherever he went. His clothes often broke the ice on a cold turkey interview. Several prospects asked him where he had purchased the clothes and requested the address of the London tailor or haberdasher. Invariably this led to contracts and Lyle became one of the top earners of his firm. Many of his customers called him "The Englishman" although he was born in Kansas City.

The British appearance gave this man style and distinction. He was only a little better than average salesman, but he knew how to capitalize on a good thing. He pocketed many orders on the strength of his appearance alone. Buyers were flattered that such an elegant gentleman had come seeking their business.

These are only some of the ways by which a salesman can brighten his impression. A racy-looking sports car, for example, can polish up the salesman's luster. If the auto is fire engine

red so much the better. He'll be known as the guy who drives
the "flashy foreign job."

Stop Short of Vulgarity and Unnaturalness

Please don't misunderstand me. I'm not advocating that a
salesman become loud or vulgar to grab attention. Such tactics
will lose more customers than they'll win. Nor do I suggest that
the salesman try to alter his basic personality—that is, to become
something he is not by nature.

What I do urge is that the salesman work out some way to
give himself a distinctive image—an image that will cause a
prospect or buyer to take a second look. A little thought and
imagination can accomplish wonders if the individual will only
try.

During World War II millions of American G.I.'s chafed
under the conformity and regimentation of the military services.
They longed for the day when they could again wear bright
colors, sleep late and go their own way.

Yet, for most of them after the war, the opportunity was
squandered. Drab greys and browns proved to be the most
popular colors in suits. Instead of sleeping late they caught the
7:43 from Stamford or Evanston. Once in the city, the veterans
joined thousands of others who looked exactly like them.

From a distance, they looked like an army of ants marching in
ranks.

This "civilian conformity" carried over to their jobs and attitudes. "Let's not do anything different," seemed to be their
motto. Grey flannel became the uniform of the white collar
worker from Madison Avenue to Houston.

The conformity even extended to the homes of the veterans.
Vast suburban tracts were developed with millions of homes
that differed only in the name on the mailbox.

Selling also remained locked in old concepts. Few were bold

enough to experiment with new ideas and methods. But those who did were able to reap rich rewards.

A truly new idea is a valuable commodity on the market. This applies to salesmen as well as to the selling process. The salesman, who can make himself recognized, is an asset to himself and his organization. Sales managers look for men who will not merely cover a territory but will be creative. It takes more than a good product to sell a prospect.

First Impressions Count

Selling often revolves around the personal relationship between buyer and seller. This rapport is much easier to obtain if the salesman has made a firm impression on the mind of the customer.

One can always tell the salesman who has made a dramatic impression by the reception he gets on the second call.

If the prospect has forgotten his name and can't even remember his face, the impression was negative.

To register positively on buyers, the salesman must punch through with some idea or talent that will differentiate him from the hundreds of other salesmen calling on that prospect. The old adage "alike as two peas in a pod" can be applied to selling. The salesman who is afraid to bridge convention must resign himself to a life of mediocrity.

Most of us have the potential for success. It's the way we use it that counts. Or, I should say, the way we don't use it.

Don't be afraid to be different.

All successful people are.

23

Ducking Dissatisfied Customers

THERE'S ONLY ONE WAY TO MEET A DISSATISFIED CUS
tomer: head on!

The salesman who avoids this responsibility is doing serious
damage to himself and his company. None of us like unpleasant
tasks, but this is one that must be met, and met promptly. If the
salesman delays, the dissatisfaction, like an untreated wound,
will fester and cause more trouble.

Yet many salesmen won't tackle a customer's gripe. They
keep putting it off, hoping it will somehow all blow away. This
is childish thinking. And expensive. Millions of dollars in accounts are lost every year because salesmen won't investigate
customer dissatisfaction and take steps to eliminate it.

The Problem Is Often Minor

The reason for the customer's unhappiness with a particular
firm is often easily traceable and remedied. Sometimes it is
based on nothing more than a misunderstanding. Lack of
proper communication on the matter has widened the gulf between the company and the customer.

But some salesmen create imaginary fears that the problem can never be licked. Instead of facing up to the customer dissatisfaction, they timidly retreat from it. Finally, they manage to stop thinking about it.

A good example occurred in my own marketing consulting business.

The sales manager of one of our client firms threw what he thought was a curve at us. We had disagreed on sales methods during a prolonged discussion in his office. Suddenly he asked pointblank.

"Can you get Saks Fifth Avenue on our books?"

"Yes, if you have a product they will buy," I responded quickly. Actually, I wasn't that sure of myself, but I have found in selling its always better to say yes.

The sales manager's firm manufactured high quality lingerie. The company's customers included Bonwit Teller, Lord & Taylor and other fine shops. However, the man was strangely evasive when we tried to find out why Saks was not among its outlets since the firm's merchandise seemed to fit ideally into that kind of store.

My son, Bruce, was curious enough to do a little sleuthing on his own. The next day he went to the office of Saks' lingerie buyer and put the question to her directly.

The woman was surprised by the approach, but more than happy to explain. She informed Bruce that Saks once gave our client business amounting to $100,000 a year.

Then one day the buyer and the sales manager for our client had an argument. Saks cancelled the business and the rift had never been patched up

"What was tne spat about?" Bruce asked.

"I've forgotten," she shrugged. "It was some trifling matter, but neither one of us would take the first step to straighten it out so here we are."

The woman admitted our client carried a good line that would be a credit to Saks.

"Please do me a favor," Bruce asked. "Jump in a taxi with me and we'll go down right now and see the sales manager."

She agreed and the whole affair was put to rights that same afternoon.

The Original Problem Is Magnified by Time

Later, the sales manager was pretty sheepish about the whole thing. He confessed he had used us to pull his chestnuts out of the fire because he was afraid to do it himself.

"But why?" I demanded. "The entire business was much ado about nothing. You could have gotten back in Saks' good graces in 10 minutes."

"I know that now," he conceded, "but the longer I put it off, the more certain I became there wasn't a chance to get the order back."

Our client not only got the original business back, but surpassed it by a big margin.

Here was a sales manager who let thousands and thousands of dollars of business go down the drain because he couldn't overcome the embarrassment of admitting he was wrong, or, at least, making some move toward resolving the bitterness.

That's a high price to pay for pride.

Similar situations can be found in almost any territory. Old feuds, misunderstandings and petty grievances are permitted to linger for months and years with no attempt to get at the root of them. The customer remains dissatisfied and business is lost.

There also are cases where the competition, using unethical tactics, has created harm that a salesman must take years to undo.

An old friend of mine, Gordon Haley, was the victim of just such circumstances. A smart and conscientious salesman, Gordon took a job with a firm that was selling housewares to department stores throughout the country. The assignment was something new to him. Previously, he had sold the same line in a single territory for another manufacturer.

Gordon had expected the job to be a challenge, but he was completely unprepared for the discouraging reception he got on almost all his calls.

He encountered one dissatisfied customer after another. Most of them treated him like a pariah.

Gordon was hurt and mystified. He had a good reputation for honesty and integrity. His former employer had given him the best references. He also was aware of the fact that he presently worked for a reputable outfit that sold a good product. Why then the deep freeze from prospects and customers?

One day a customer took pity on Gordon and gave him the full story on why his territory was "jinxed." He learned that his predecessor had done a thorough job of running down the company before he left to operate his own business. He and a partner were going to produce the same line and he was doing some advance salesmanship. Each company has vulnerable spots and this man knew it. He did everything he could to discredit the firm he was supposed to be representing. And he continued the process when he became sales manager for his own organization.

You can see Gordon started with quite a handicap. Unfortunately, many buyers, who should know better, are ready to believe the worst about a company without having all the facts. Most of them had swallowed whole every bit of bad publicity the other man had spread about Gordon's firm.

My friend realized, however, that there was no point in picking a fight with the other fellow or shedding tears over the trouble he had caused. There was only one thing to do, he decided: Turn every dissatisfied customer into a satisfied one.

Instead of being embarrassed or apologetic about the gripe, Gordon met it head on. He produced facts that proved many of the complaints were unfounded. When the grumble was justified, he saw that it was corrected, always calling the matter to the company's attention. Whether it was a matter of production, price, delivery, service or promotion, he made sure someone did something about it.

Gordon did not waste time trying to damage the other salesman's reputation. He didn't even mention him. His sole purpose was to tackle each complaint, determine its validity and then take action. Sometimes it required no more than an earnest chat with the buyer to convince him he had been misinformed.

It took a few years, but Gordon brought every dissatisfied customer into line. At the same time, he earned a reputation for himself that carried him to the top in his field.

Sometime after this incident, Gordon learned from his firm's vice president that he had been handpicked for the job.

"We knew all about the practices of your predecessor, but we didn't tell you because we wanted you to start off without any preconditioning by us," the executive told Gordon.

Because of his prompt, sensible handling of that assignment, Gordon became a highly paid trouble-shooter for the firm. Whenever a territory is plagued with dissatisfied customers who can't be mollified, Gordon is dispatched there to smooth it over. Many of the salesmen in those territories have learned from him that letting a bad situation drag on only makes it worse. His advice to the men is to take the initiative every time.

The First Move Is up to the Salesman

"The first move is up to the salesman," Gordon tells them. "A customer who is dissatisfied in the morning can be your loyal friend by afternoon if you handle him right."

Customer dissatisfaction may spring from many causes—company policies, late deliveries, personality difficulty with a salesman and buyer, the supplier's relationship with competitors and others. But whatever the reason, the rift must be healed and good will restored. This is a prime requisite for high production in any territory.

It's a mistake to overcome customer dissatisfaction by rapping the competition, even when they sow false rumors and reports that hurt you.

The customer is likely to think you are using the competition as an alibi to cover up your company's mistakes. Act as if you had never heard that the competition was responsible for the customer's poor opinion of your firm. Take the complaint for what it's worth and deal with it as your responsibility.

Another mistake is to attempt to counteract the opposition's mudslinging with a few tosses of your own. It isn't worth it. In the first place, customers and prospects resent such tactics. Second, the prospect may be a user of the competitor's product and will probably defend it to back his own judgment. Finally, why waste your breath knocking the competition when you should be saving it to sell your own product?

There also is no point in blaming other salesmen in your firm or someone in the home office when a customer complains. The latter is not dealing with them; he is dealing with you and expects the answer from you. Buck-passing is not a game that salesmen should play in handling customer gripes.

A salesman will win respect and admiration if he quietly goes about removing obstacles that block sales and good will. Erasing customer dissatisfaction is a salesman's responsibility.

Don't duck the problem. It will be there waiting for you the next time.

24

Seeking Miracles in a Broader Line

SOME SALESMEN ARE PRONE TO FIND EXCUSES FOR THEIR low volume and earnings. They are quick to blame everything and everybody when the going gets tough. That is, everybody but themselves. One of the most frequent alibis is that the product line is not big enough. The competition is showing more merchandise, they complain.

"Just give me more items and things will be different," the salesman promises his boss.

The latter, who has given as little thought to the idea as the salesman, readily agrees because he trusts the man's judgment. Then both await the miracle they are sure will follow. Most of the time the wait is in vain.

A Common Scapegoat

This is a common mistake of salesmen—the untested belief that a wider product line is a panacea for poor earnings.

The fact is that by taking on extra products, the salesman often finds himself in a worse fix than he was before.

One man who maneuvered himself into this position was Arch Campbell, who sold window hardware to jobbers. At sales meetings Arch attended, he always heard one or two men plead for more products to offset the competition's advantage in this department. Arch was rather new with the firm and at first didn't express an opinion on the subject. But, after a while, the other salesmen began to sound so convincing and knowing that they infected him with their enthusiasm for an expanded line. The others, incidentally, were doing poorly in their territories.

So a few meetings later, Arch added his voice to the request for more products. He had been having a difficult time getting started and this seemed the answer to his problem.

The company eventually gave in and soon Arch was carrying 72 items instead of his normal 50. At the end of a year Arch was a sad and disillusioned man. He was actually doing less business than he had with the smaller line and there was no prospect of improvement.

What had happened was this:

Competitors, realizing that Arch's company was spreading itself too thin, moved in with one or two highly specialized items at a good price and knocked the props from under his entire line.

Diversification Creates Its Own Problems

The diversification on which Arch and others had placed so much faith actually became an albatross around their necks. His line was so broad that he was unable to concentrate on any one item and consequently spent a lot of useless energy trying to do justice to each one.

The worst damage was to his morale. Arch became frustrated and bitter and even thought of giving up selling.

Finally, he dumped the problem in the lap of his supervisors who dumped it right back.

"This is what you wanted," one company executive reminded

Arch. "You guys begged us to widen your line so you could meet the competition. We went along because we thought you had the right answer. The extra items cost the firm money and time."

Arch was forced to eat crow, but he learned something he was never to forget. Instead of crying any longer over the situation, he re-traced his steps to see where he went wrong.

His research showed him that while his outfit was branching out, its competitors were narrowing their lines at a profit. They were able to make their prices more attractive while his firm was forced to raise its prices because of increased production costs brought on by the expansion.

What's more, here was no economic law that said product expansion meant more business.

Arch realized that some of the most prosperous firms in the country concentrated on one or two products. One company, for example, produced only baking soda and yet commanded a nation-wide market. It's true that General Electric and Westinghouse manufacture a tremendous range of electrical products, but few companies are in that league.

Since Arch had been partly responsible for his outfit's bad policy, he determined to make amends. At the next sales meeting he suggested a complete reversal of the trend toward product extension.

"For the past five years," he declared, "we have followed a tactic of increasing our line almost every year. It has gotten us nowhere. In fact, we have weakened our position in every territory we cover.

"Many of us are guilty of leading management down the wrong road to cover up our own inadequacies as salesmen. We failed in our responsibility. When we got in a hole we asked the company to puff up our line instead of doing a better job with what we had. We have a damn good product if we'll get in there and sell it."

Arch suggested that the line never be stretched out unless at least three-fourths of the salesmen approve, and that the approval be backed by a marketing survey.

The plan was adopted and every salesman on the force benefited.

A Narrow Line Has Many Advantages

They divested themselves of the myth that more products mean more sales and faced the cold fact that selling power depends on more than simply offering the prospect a huge grab bag.

The company's salesmen now fight to reduce the line rather than expand it. The payoff is that prices and quality are better, deliveries more efficient and there are fewer complaints. Arch's income also improved considerably, along with that of his colleagues.

With a smaller family of products, the salesmen were able to learn more about them for telling sales presentations and demonstrations. They knew exactly what the products would and would not do and every detail about them. They also were able to concentrate more fully on the needs and special problems of customers and prospects.

Most important, the new policy created a more favorable climate for the salesmen and management. The salesmen, who had been inclined to think of their bosses as whipping boys for their own failures, realized that success in selling depends on understanding and complete faith between the man and his company.

Salesmen, in many respects, are the eyes and ears of their organizations. Management, stuck in the home office, cannot be expected to have personal knowledge of a territory.

So company officials rely on the salesman's advice in many instances. Before attempting to guide his firm, however, the salesman should carefully consider the whole picture. It may be that at times a new product is indicated. The salesman, who feels this need, should remember that he is covering only one segment of the market. Therefore, it is better if he approaches management with some caution.

He might, for example, say to his sales manager:

"There seems to be room in my territory for more widgets in our line. I thought perhaps you might want to toss the idea to the other salesmen for their opinions or have our marketing people make a survey."

This shows a responsible attitude by the salesman and at the same time enables him to avoid being the goat if the suggestion is a flop.

Such clear thinking acts as a brake on the tendency of some salesmen to rush headlong into a venture without first examining all its aspects and giving it mature consideration. Guard against being panicked into an action you might later regret.

Quality Pulls More Weight than Quantity

A young salesman I know, Pat Morley, was dismayed one day when a prospect told him: "A man from the XYZ Company was in here the other day with a line twice the size of yours and was selling at a lower price."

Pat handled a line of precision cutting instruments that were as good or better than any produced in the world. They were of the finest steel and made to such exact specifications that the firm's rejects were superior to most other brands.

Pat had been told all this during his indoctrination and training, but it all washed away when he heard the prospect. All he could think of was that he was working at a terrible disadvantage to his competition.

After gathering all the information about the rival line, he hurried back to his sales manager and reported his awesome discovery. The sales manager was unimpressed.

"Look, Pat," he replied calmly, "we know all about the XYZ firm and its line. They make an inferior product and its new products are equally bad. The purchasing agent you talked to is a new man and isn't aware yet of that company's reputation.

"It's true we have a smaller line, but it's one which serves the needs of our customers who know our instruments perform better and last longer."

The sales manager then took Pat over the various stages of product research and development, manufacture, quality control, and distribution.

Pat returned to his territory with a completely new viewpoint, one which enabled him to shrug off competing lines by the secure knowledge that his products, although narrower in variety, were vastly superior.

Pat invited customers of competing products to make comparative tests with his own and even contributed his own time to helping with the tests. The results proved conclusively that he offered the better value for the money.

What Do You Do with It When You Get It?

In examining the different facets of expanded lines, I also have found that many salesmen don't know what to do with a new product when they do get it. They're so used to concentrating on the old ones they fail to point up the fresh addition to the line. This is another mistake.

The prospect has a natural curiosity about new things, if only the salesman will satisfy it. Even if the salesman has had the product for some time, it's still new to the buyer if he hasn't seen it.

Often the salesman neglects to talk about new items because he feels an obligation to continue pushing the existing products which have served him so well. He also is fearful that the new product may not go over well and possibly undermine his success with the old ones.

He should rid himself of this bugaboo. Selling is, above all, dynamic and creative. New products, new ideas and new selling methods are challenges he should meet with open arms. A new product today may be your most successful item in six months. If a salesman can break down his own resistance to the new item, it's only a question of time before he sells the prospect on it.

One sales manager I know breaks the ice for a new product by accompanying the salesman on his first trip with the item. This has the double advantage of lending prestige to the merchandise by the presence of the executive and of giving the salesman the necessary moral support.

This same manager has also toured the territory with salesmen who complained that their line wasn't big enough to meet competition. The supervisor, by a thorough presentation of the man's wares, was able to beat the competition hands down.

All this points up three basic factors in selling:

1. The salesman must sell himself before he sells the product—new or old.
2. A good product and a dynamic sales presentation are usually enough to offset the competitor's expanded line.
3. A broadened line in itself is no assurance of increased sales and earnings.

Before you ask your company for more products, make sure you are doing a proper job in selling the ones you have.

25

Ignoring Small Orders

HARRY DASH DOESN'T LIKE TO BE BOTHERED WITH SMALL orders.

When he writes one up he acts as if he's doing a big favor for the customer at the cost of his valuable time. Like many other salesmen weaned on fat post-war business, Harry is strictly a big ticket man.

He's also shortsighted.

Let's examine Harry's philosophy.

He figures that the only payoff for his time and effort is in the value of an order. He knows, for example, that a $300 order will net him six percent or $18, so why trouble himself.

Harry may have made $2,000 on the stock market that week or picked up a $15,000 order from an important customer. In either case, he calculates he would have to call on 200 lesser accounts to get as much money, so he passes them up.

This is a mistake on two counts.

No Man Is an Island

First, Harry doesn't stop to realize that 50 percent of that $300 order goes into the pockets of the people who backstop him—the producers, shipping clerks, bookkeepers, administrators, foremen, etc.

These persons are important to Harry. The old saying that no man is an island is especially true of salesmen.

During World War II it was estimated that five rear echelon men were needed to support each combat soldier at the front. These were the personnel who supplied the food, ammunition, medicine clothing and other material. Without them, the infantryman was helpless.

So it is with the salesman. His success depends on the support and good will of the people on the production and distribution front. Suppose the factory fouled up Harry's orders, didn't deliver them on time, or gave second-class treatment to an order just because it was small. Harry would blow his top—and with good reason. He takes it for granted that he'll get the proper logistic support.

The salesman simply isn't being fair to his company by ignoring or slighting small orders. He's part of an organization that will prosper or perish on the strength of how well each member does his job. In fact, the smart salesman will show his appreciation to the home office gang by sending a note of thanks for a particularly fine job of backing him up. He lets them know how important they are to his success.

These acknowledgments mean a lot to those "rear echelon" crewmen. Everybody likes a pat on the back for a job well done.

Little Fish Grow to Be Big Fish

The second mistake in passing up the small order hits directly at the salesman's income. Quite often a little customer can become a big one through better selling or simply as the result of circumstances.

Bill Elwell patiently solicited for years a small customer who knew that Bill's company did most of its business in the community with one large firm.

Even so, the little customer was flattered and pleased by Bill's regular appearance to pick up his tiny order.

One day he asked Bill: "Why do you keep coming around when there is so little in it for you and your company?"

The firm was buying a certain metal used for anvils.

"Because you are a regular customer and deserve whatever attention I can give you," Bill replied. This was just before World War II.

About a month later as Bill showed up on schedule, the head of the firm called him into his office.

"Bill," he announced, "I've got a surprise for you. We have just obtained a big government contract to produce turrets for battleships. You were faithful to us during the lean years, and now we're going to make it up to you in substantial orders."

That little New England plant became a multi-million dollar corporation and Bill a $50,000-a-year man. Luck? Partly, but remember that company president just didn't hand over the business to the first salesman who walked in the door. Bill largely made his own break by laying a solid foundation of good will and loyalty all those years.

Another friend of mine, Ken Jurgis, was given a territory in northern Illinois and Wisconsin by a big food company when he was still a young man. About every month Ken used to go out of his way to service a one-man grocery store just because he liked to talk hunting with the owner.

Well, the man's two sons were growing up and they eventually built up that store into a huge supermarket. In a few years they had a chain of markets throughout the Mid-West. The boys remembered Ken's friendship with their father and made him one of the richest salesmen in the country.

Naturally this won't happen with all small concerns but every salesman should be alert to future possibilities.

Establish a Priority System for Calls

To bring home this point, suppose we classify customers this way: The "A" group are your most important customers. You call on them once a month and they rate the attention of your top brass at various times.

The "B" group are good substantial buyers you visit every other month. They deserve and should get close attention.

The "C" group are your least profitable customers. Most of them are small and account for only a fraction of your income. Maybe you call on them two or three times a year.

Now the salesman who skips or drops the "C" customer could be making a serious mistake, even though he is handling the account at little profit. For one thing, he puts himself, his company and the customer in a vulnerable position. His competitor can pick off the account, his company loses business and prestige, and, in the long run, the salesman is very likely to hurt himself financially.

Look at the situation this way: Today's "C" buyer may be in the "B" or "A" group tomorrow. When this happens, the salesman who couldn't be bothered with the small order will find it almost impossible to win back the account. Most likely, his competition will have taken it over. Remember, many of today's blue chip "A" firms were once in the "B" and "C" categories. One only has to study the phenomenal growth of some companies since World War II to realize this.

You Can Help the Customer to Grow

Of course, the salesman and his company have to make a profit, but no salesman should overlook the potentialities of a customer who may not be pulling his weight at the moment. He should explore and analyze his district for small customers who can be made more profitable through smarter selling or who have within themselves the elements of growth.

This process may involve writing off a few customers with no foreseeable potential, but that's part of a salesman's job. In other words, the seller doesn't have to play nursemaid to every small dealer in his area. He can and should be selective. Take the case of Cliff Underhill.

Cliff inherited a territory with a few really sizable accounts and a flock of small ones. He knew the latter could provide his "bread and butter" volume, but he also realized it would be better for him and his company if he weeded out the deadwood.

So he classified the small customers into two groups—the promising and the unpromising, giving the former most of the time and attention he had available for lesser accounts. That time was broken up according to how many such customers he had, how often they bought, and how often he could help them. However, most of his effort with small customers went into trying to turn them into big ones. He worked with them in arranging attractive displays, gave them merchandising ideas and passed on new sales techniques.

It wasn't long before some of Cliff's "C" customers became "B" and even "A" users. Others were scratched off his list entirely as far as calls were concerned. Cliff found it more practical and economical to service them by mail unless an unusual situation arose.

Cliff was well aware that his competitors would have been only too happy to grab off accounts he let slip away.

Most salesmen find that after a few years in a territory most of their business comes from 20 percent of their accounts. They will do a strong job on this group while giving the other 80 percent the once-over-lightly treatment. This is a perfect setup for a rival to woo away the 80 percent with aggressive salesmanship and then go after the 20 percent. Selling is not static. You can be sailing along comfortably one day and be torpedoed the next.

Constant Care Keeps Customers

But, other things being equal, a customer will not switch over to a competitor if he has been getting proper care and attention from a salesman. Customers are people, not merely names in your files. They know when they're being treated right—and they know when they're not. No dealer wants to feel that a salesman is doing him a big favor by taking his order. In his own eyes and in others he is an important member of the community. Through the years he has created good will, respect and loyalty among *his* customers. Imagine his feeling when some salesman turns up his nose at a small order. He is likely never to forget it.

Keep after those small orders. If you give them proper nourishment they will grow into big ones. Besides, you owe it to your company and all the people standing behind you to gather all the business you can. More than your welfare is at stake.

It's fine to think big, but it's even more important to think clearly. Don't make the mistake of throwing away the small order before you consider the harm you may be doing yourself and your firm.

26

Forgetting the Company's Showroom

A POPULAR MISCONCEPTION IS THAT SALESMEN LACK sensitivity. Nothing is farther from the truth.

They are extremely sensitive to criticism from their supervisors, customers and even other salesmen. Tell a salesman that he could do a better job if he changed some of his habits and you've got an argument. Yet many salesmen can benefit from helpful advice that would alter their perspective and lead to greater profits.

One fixed idea that needs revision is the conviction of many salesmen that all their selling must be done on the road. Their mistake lies in not realizing that their home office showroom can often sell for them.

This fixation involves what sales expert Robert E. Moore calls the "sacred cows" of selling. The theory is that salesmen are satisfied with certain methods mostly because they are comfortable and familiar. They've been doing it that way for so long it must be right, they argue. These habits are sacred cows that cannot be touched.

Let's undermine the sacred cow idea that all the salesman's business should be done in the field.

Disadvantages of Field Selling

For one thing, field selling has certain built-in disadvantages every salesman encounters. He often has to show his line in badly lighted and stuffy hotel rooms. Showing the product in a store can be an equally dismal experience. There is little room for display and often the operation is rushed because the dealer is busy with customers. An air conditioner salesman I know, Clint Baker, once had to spend a day in a small midwestern town because a certain retailer couldn't find time to talk to him.

"It was horrible," Clint recalled. "I returned to the store four or five times trying to do business but each time the owner was tied up. Then I'd go out for coffee. By late afternoon I had drunk so much coffee it was spilling out my ears. When I finally did get his attention it was too late for a good presentation. I squeezed out a token order but I really lost money that day."

Any salesman can have a bad day but Clint's ordeal is not uncommon. Much of this can be avoided by urging the retailer or dealer to visit the company showroom the next time he is in New York, Chicago or Los Angeles. No one, least of all the salesman's boss, will complain that he is lying down on the job or passing the buck in letting the house do the actual selling. On the contrary, management *expects* this kind of cooperation from its field men and will often reward them with a bonus above their regular commission for their imaginative thinking in directing prospects to the home office.

Benefits of Selling at Home

The headquarters' reaction is understandable when you consider these benefits to showroom selling:

1. The customer gets to see the *entire* line at the showroom. Salesmen are limited to what they can carry.

2. The showroom is built and geared to present the product to the best possible advantage. Handsome fixtures, attractive display cases, tasteful decor and flattering lighting all contribute to whetting the buyer's appetite. In the fashion line, lovely models add a gracious touch.

3. The buyer is impressed by the personal attention of the company president, vice president or sales chief. This is the prestige factor.

4. Company executives get closer to the dealers' problems and at the same time get a sharper focus on the total market picture.

5. The salesman gets the benefit of headquarters experts such as advertising managers, display men and promotion specialists, who can advise and guide the buyer on his special needs. No salesman can be an expert in all these fields.

6. There is more time for selling. The customer is in town primarily for one purpose—to buy. Once in the show-room there are no distractions. He can relax in a comfortable chair, smoke a cigarette and make a leisurely choice. *He is in a buying mood.* Salesmen seldom get such a receptive audience.

Keep in mind that dealers, particularly large ones, make one or more buying trips a year. The big markets are only hours away from the remotest hamlet and such a journey gives the prospect a chance to combine business with pleasure. He is likely to have a list of eight or ten houses he plans to visit. It's the salesman's duty to make sure that his company is on that list.

A salesman who thinks on his feet will wire his office to expect Joe Merrill from Kenosha on a particular day so the red carpet can be laid out. This pleases both the customer and the company brass. The former is grateful to the salesman for setting up the appointment and the boss is happy over the prospect of a substantial order. After all, there is a lot of selling talent back at headquarters. Why shouldn't the salesman use it?

Teamwork

Field and showroom selling are not separate operations. Actually, they go hand in hand.

The president of the country's second largest costume jewelry company told me:

"Selling in our New York office and selling on the road are tied together. On trips, our salesmen are expected to raise the interest pitch of the prospect so he will come here and see our complete line in the right surroundings.

"In our showroom, selling is strictly a business proposition as compared to the more personal contact on the road. But we find that buyers coming here want it that way.

"There's little lost motion and in an hour we can often accomplish more than a field man in three or four hours with a customer."

The executive noted, however, that back in his hometown, the buyer wants the close, personal relationship with the salesman.

"This is what I mean by showroom and road selling working together," he explained. "The salesman lays the groundwork for the customer's visit to us."

New York doesn't have a monopoly on showrooms. Firms in Chicago, Milwaukee, Kansas City, Minneapolis, San Francisco and other cities offer first-rate display facilities.

I recently met a Milwaukee men's wear manufacturer who began his career as a salesman.

"In the early days," he recalled, "I was on the road and my brother ran the office. We didn't even have a showroom by that name and we didn't need one. Out-of-town buying was a luxury my customers never even thought of. Today we've got a $30,000 display room that's busy every hour of the day.

"We do a tremendous volume here and all because our salesmen are on the ball. Practically every customer we get here has been sent by one of our boys."

A veteran salesman, who has been on the road since 1933 with a lingerie line, told me of the high cost of selling.

"My expenses run as high as $150 a week for renting hotel suites and other things," he said.

"I can eliminate much of this cost by referring the prospect to the home office where he can see more of the line under better conditions. My commission is the same."

You Will Not Lose Sales

Some salesmen hesitate to push the showroom for fear of losing sales. This is nonsense. Experience has shown that sales will increase on a territorial basis if the prospect is convinced of the merits of showroom buying.

The sales manager for a women's apparel firm stresses at every sales meeting the importance of getting buyers to visit the showroom when they are in town.

One of his men, Vince Roselle, was so impressed by the speech that he worked full time at being kind of a roving ambassador for his outfit. After a few years, 75 percent of his sales were made in the showroom. Vince, operating as a good will emissary, spent most of his road time merely shaking hands with customers and pointing them in the direction of New York.

"There's no sense in my showing you 10 things when you can see 300 in company headquarters," he told them.

Eventually Vince was promoted to vice president of sales, then sales manager and finally vice president of marketing for the entire organization. Today he devotes a sizable share of his time to selling salesmen on the value of their "personal showroom."

Getting the Smaller Prospect to Travel

A crucial task for the salesman is educating the small and medium buyer to come to the home office. Department stores and other big customers have staffs of trained buyers who travel periodically to the main markets and know all the angles of competition.

The small customer is less sophisticated. To him a buying trip to New York or Chicago is a major undertaking. For one thing he has to go himself which means leaving his business in the hands of a store manager or clerk. He also is apt to feel like the proverbial little frog in the big pond when he gets to the city. He's a bit nervous about the whole thing.

The field man must erase these doubts. Tell him he'll be welcome even if he doesn't spend a dime. But the salesman must be sure he is backed up by his office. It would be disastrous if he couldn't deliver on such a promise.

Some companies break the ice by paying the expenses of good customers invited to headquarters.

"We figure it's well worth it," declared the sales manager of one of the nation's largest hardware companies. "We not only bring him here but we wine and dine him as well. To us it's an investment that pays off in sales."

The same firm offers a fat bonus to the salesman responsible for steering the prospect to the home office.

Still, old habits are hard to break for many salesmen. When I tried to convert one man to showroom selling, he shot back:

"Look, I carry catalogues that list in detail every item my outfit handles.

"Every other salesman worth his salt has similar material. What's the point of lugging this stuff around if we don't use it for on-the-spot selling? We can bring the showroom to the prospect."

Showmanship and Drama of the HQ

"No you can't," I retorted. "Your catalogues are fine but you can't duplicate the showmanship and drama the customer gets at headquarters. You can't let him see each and every product in a rich and harmonious setting. You can't produce your top executives to impress him. And besides, you have nothing to lose and everything to gain by promoting the showroom."

I finally persuaded him to give the idea a trial. A few weeks later we met again and I asked him how it had worked out.

"Great," he exclaimed. "I had been trying for months to interest one customer in a particular item. (He sold glassware.) On my last trip I learned he was going to Chicago and I invited him to drop into our office. In the showroom he spotted that item in a beautiful table setting and liked it so much he bought several gross."

I can't guarantee that kind of success with every prospect, but you're not being fair to yourself or your company if you don't at least give the showroom a chance.

What have you got to lose? Even the most palatial showrooms won't eliminate the need for salesmen. Think of the showroom as a new tool that can broaden you horizon and your income.

It's a mistake if you don't.

27

Not Plugging Your Company's Prestige

BROADWAY AND HOLLYWOOD BOX OFFICE APPEAL OFTEN depends on the star or stars heading the cast.

A big name actor or actress can extend the run of a mediocre or even bad play or movie. They can turn a good one into a smashing success.

Producers spend enormous sums of money to exploit these artists in billboard, newspaper and magazine advertisements. Their names are emblazoned in huge type, dwarfing the title of the play itself.

Publicists are, of course, aware of the magnetism of these names. No opportunity is lost to build up the prestige of the play or picture by stressing the reputations of its highpowered performers.

Don't Assume Prospect Knows Your Company

Many salesmen make the mistake of not promoting what may be the real star of *their* performance—the company they represent. All too frequently, the salesman takes the reputation of his firm for granted and assumes the prospect will also. This is a fatal assumption for these reasons:

146

1. His is not the only prominent outfit in the field.
2. Even though his organization may be outstanding, it does not necessarily follow that everyone knows about it. This is a big country.
3. The prestige of his company fits so naturally into the sales talk that it's a shame not to use it.
4. If he doesn't blow the horn for this firm, the buyer may wonder why.
5. He can be sure his competitors are trading on their company's reputation.
6. The prestige factor makes the proposition more believable and interesting.

Working for a "name" outfit can produce a feeling of smugness on the part of the salesman. His attitude is: "Why emphasize the obvious?" The company's standing is only obvious if the salesman makes it so. And even if the prospect knows the seller's reputation, he won't know the whole company story.

Reputation Is Part of the Product's Price

The supplier's good name is doubly important in the matter of price competition.

My files contain the illuminating case history of a heating equipment salesman named Pete Armstrong. Pete's firm had been in business for 70 years and had justly earned its fine reputation. But time had produced several other well managed, reliable companies. The latters' products could not match those of Pete's outfit, but they were high quality—and they were cheaper.

Pete was up against a tough obstacle. He knew he had a better product, but he couldn't seem to capitalize on this difference in his presentation. The competition began making serious inroads into his volume and earnings

Now Pete's son happened to be a brilliant high school basketball player. Scores of colleges tried to recruit him, offering the boy every sort of inducement, including four years of free tuition and room and board.

The recruiter who got Pete's son offered something more important. He minimized athletic scholarships and stressed instead the reputation of the university he represented. The lad would not only play basketball but would receive an outstanding education to prepare him for later life, Pete was told.

The argument proved the deciding factor and it also gave Pete an idea for his territory. He decided to embark on a program to wipe out the price differential of his competitors by making his product seem more attractive to the prospects. To accomplish this, he used a reserve source that was there for him all along.

First, he conducted an informal survey which revealed that a number of his prospects were rather unfamiliar with his outfit. Although his company had been a leader for years, his prospective customers had undergone sweeping changes in personnel during that time. Most of the old timers who had known his firm had died off. Their replacements, younger men, had only sketchy knowledge of his company's reputation for honesty, integrity and fair play.

Pete set out to educate the newcomers. He began by soaking up all the information he could get about his own organization. He spent hours talking to production men and other officials who had been with the firm 30 or 40 years. He learned, even to his own surprise, the many things his company had done to earn its esteem.

He discovered, for example, that during World War II, his firm had allocated its products fairly to all its customers, despite the fact that it could have made millions by supplying only the bigger ones. He was told, too, that his outfit had frequently carried a customer on the books until he got out of financial difficulty. One executive recalled that the firm had once withdrawn $200,000 worth of merchandise that was faulty because of poor raw material. The company took a deep finan-cial loss to protect its customers. Pete memorized these facts and wove them into his sales talk. He now sold himself, the product and his *company*.

His prospects listened. They were impressed by the firm's record of fairness and straight dealing with customers. They realized it would be good business to buy from such a firm, even at a slightly higher price. After all, they reasoned, the product was superior and, in the event of shortages or an emergency, Pete's firm could be relied upon not to let them down. In a sense, they were buying peace of mind, along with the merchandise. This is an intangible product, but an im-portant one.

Know Your Company History

Knowing vital information about his company should be high on the list of a salesman's attributes. The prestige of your firm may mean the difference between getting an order or losing it.

This means that every salesman should become a public re-lations agent for his own outfit. Company distinction makes potent ammunition if properly used. Be proud of your com-pany and sell the prospect on this pride. But remember, you must be sold on your firm before you can sell the prospect.

Some companies furnish their salesmen with narrative ac-counts of their achievements, awards and contributions to society or their communities. The Hershey Chocolate Com-pany tells its salesmen of the many donations and benefits Mr. Hershey heaped on the town of Hershey, Pennsylvania.

Such information may not be of direct significance to the prospect, but it helps make the salesman's presentation more colorful and interesting.

Sources and Types of Information

Lyle Tremaine, a photo-engraving equipment salesman, carefully culls the trade magazines for news about his company. In the past several years, his firm has won international honors for its new processes and other advances. All this is meat for Lyle, who makes sure his prospects are advised of these awards.

Other salesmen work into their presentations the wealth, affluenc. or diversification of their organizations. Prospects consider this essential business information. The salesman should know his company's earning record, equipment, key personnel in production and research, various plants, holdings and other products. Very often he will be asked these questions.

I know an industrial lighting salesman who carries beautiful, glossy pictures of the interior and exterior of his home office and factory. The illustrations are designed to give the prospect a feeling of confidence in and respect for the company.

Anything which can enhance reputation, character or efficiency of the company should be exploited by the salesman. Don't make the mistake of thinking that your firm's fame has preceded you. You've got to beat the drums and beat them hard to impress this fact on the prospect.

I can think of one salesman who learned his lesson in an embarrassing but effective way. Jim Akers, who represented a well-established firm, was inclined to be somewhat cocky on his calls. One day he was interviewing the crusty head of a small but prosperous foundry in Pennsylvania. Jim was just getting into high gear when the man interrupted sharply:

"What did you say the name of your outfit was?"

Jim repeated the name.

"Never heard of you," the owner snapped and turned to some papers on his desk.

Jim flushed every color of the rainbow. He was so dumbfounded he could not continue. It was probably just as well, since the prospect had all but dismissed him.

Most prospects are more pleasant, but Jim swore this would never happen to him again. He realized his mistake. He had used his company's name as a "throwaway line" instead of really making a point of it.

Jim made it a habit to pound home his company's stature as hard as his product. He made sure at the start of the interview that the buyer understood the background and repute of his firm.

Correct Misconceptions

He picked up an extra dividend in the process. Not only was he able to acquaint prospects with his organization's standing and reputation, but, in some cases, he was able to correct mis-information some buyers had about his company. In one instance a prospect had nursed a long-standing grudge against Jim's outfit.

Jim accepted the fact calmly. However, in talking to the man, the salesman discovered the prospect's predecessor had passed the complaint on to him. In a few minutes, Jim was able to convince the buyer that the bad report was groundless. He got the order and buried forever a falsity that had been hurting his sales.

Occasionally a buyer may have a legitimate gripe against a salesman's company. A little investigation, however, may show that the complaint was valid ten, twenty or thirty years ago, but not now. The salesman who is up to date on his employer's methods, techniques, equipment, research and personnel can put the prospect's fear to rest. He can himself *create* a new and better image of his firm.

The prestige story is also important in offsetting any bad rumors or falsehoods circulated by unscrupulous competitors.

By proudly telling his company s achievements, the salesman is able to nail down the lie before it has a chance to do any damage.

Capitalize on Your Company's Special Features

The growth of a company is in itself a signpost of success. A business that sprouted from a hole-in-the-wall factory into a multi-million corporation didn't get that way through luck or guesswork. A salesman should cite this accomplishment as proof of stability, product excellence and dependability.

A highly solvent California electronics firm, with world-wide sales, began as a two-man operation in the home garage of one of the founders. The company plays up this angle in all of its promotional literature and urges its salesmen to do the same.

Bigness is nothing to be shy about. The salesman who can say "my organization is the largest of its kind in the country" will be doing himself a favor. The American success story has a lot of mileage left.

By the same token, a salesman for a small company can parlay its advantages into new orders. Impress on the prospect that the firm can process small, fill-in orders quicker and at greater profit; that it can maintain a closer, more personal relationship with the customer; that the quality of its work is finer because of tighter production supervision. Finally, the salesman might point out that, although small, his firm can match the satisfaction of its customers with that of any giant in the industry.

It's always a good idea to call the prospect's attention to the supplier's record in solving problems for other customers. A smart salesman lets his steady customers do part of his selling. There's an old adage in business that a satisfied customer is your best advertisement.

You can also raise a buyer's interest by informing him that your customers include some of the biggest names in the trade.

Many prospects wait for others to lead the way before they make a decision. If the salesman can show letters of endorsement or recommendation from customers, so much the better.

I believe the matter of company prestige is neatly summed up in the popular tune, "You've got to accentuate the positive and eliminate the negative."

Plug your firm's prestige on every call. Modesty is all right when describing your golf game, or your hunting eye, but in selling—brag, brother, brag.

28

Crying Instead of Creating

A MIDDLE SOUTH LUGGAGE MANUFACTURER MAKES IT A practice to employ handicapped workers.

He doesn't need to be sold on the idea by "Hire the Handicapped" drives nor does he act out of charity. He knows from long experience that these men and women turn out top quality work and earn every penny they're paid.

Recently, the owner took me on a tour of his plant. It was a sight I'll never forget. Some of the workers had arms and legs missing. Others were spastics and a few were totally blind. One paralytic labored while lying on his back.

Yet all performed their jobs cheerfully and competently. I picked up one finished product and found it flawless.

My host smiled.

"We get fewer rejects from this group than from our non-handicapped production personnel," he informed me.

"How come?" I asked.

"Because," he said, "this bunch didn't let themselves stay discouraged. Most of them were born with two strikes against them.

"They had to compete in a world of normal people. All of

them went through a period of bitterness and despair. But somewhere along the line they realized they had to live with their handicaps. So they made the best of them by developing skills.

"They traded discouragement for hope. They quit feeling sorry for themselves and asked for no pity."

What an inspiration!

You're Ahead When You Start

Countless salesmen with two good arms and legs make the mistake of becoming discouraged by circumstances that can be overcome by creativity, patience, persistence or extra effort. They drown in a well of self-pity, blaming "bad breaks" for their lack of production.

Nobody promised us an easy time on this earth. And only a fool or a charlatan would call selling a snap. The road to success is not downhill. It is a tough, uphill climb for the man whose goal is the top.

But it's also a well-traveled highway. Successful men in all walks of life have taken it. They didn't turn back or give up halfway because the going was too rough. Some found the necessary strength to continue within themselves. Others gained encouragement from the wise words of great men.

Take the case of Hank Morrison, who covered a western territory for a leading paint manufacturer.

When Hank first took over the territory everything went his way. There was virtually no competition and he was able to carry off a big chunk of the business in the area.

But in a few years other paint manufacturers took Horace Greeley's advice and headed their salesmen west. To catch up, the competition moved fast and soon cut deeply into Hank's volume.

Hank reached for the crying towel. It seemed so unfair to

him that the newcomers were homesteading on the territory he had pioneered.

That's business. Hank was naive. It hadn't occurred to him that, in a competitive economy, a lush district will be eventually exploited by rival firms. When the other salesmen moved in he was unprepared to deal with the situation. The competition undersold him and, in one instance, a competing supplier set up a plant in his own area. Hank's firm was 1,400 miles away. To make matters worse, his office goofed on some deliveries.

Hank's volume and earnings dropped along with his spirits. He fell so far down in the dumps he decided to quit. But he hadn't reckoned on his wife, Mary. She had faith in Hank and knew he could surmount his difficulties if only he shook off his blue funk and started fighting back.

Mary understood her husband and tried to buoy him up when he was in low spirits. When pep talks failed, she sought outside help in the form of inspiring messages from famous men who had faced adversity with courage and determination.

To get him out of his latest slump she reminded him of the words of the great British statesman, Benjamin Disraeli:

"The secret of success is constancy of purpose."

And Theodore Roosevelt:

"Far better it is to dare mighty things, to win glorious triumphs, even though checkered by failure, than to take rank with those poor spirits who neither enjoy much nor suffer much, because they live in the gray twilight that knows not victory nor defeat."

When Hank bemoaned the new competition, she drew from William Shakespeare:

"What's gone and what's past help should be past grief."

That was Mary's way of telling her husband that he was foolish to worry about a fact of life that could not be altered. The competition was there to stay. Why not meet the challenge and try to outsell and outsmart the opposition?

After Hank complained that headquarters was letting him down, Mary dipped into the thoughts of George Bernard Shaw:

"People are always blaming their circumstances for what they are. I don't believe in circumstances. The people who get on in the world are the people who get up and look for the circumstances they want, and, if they can't find them, make them."

These men, Mary explained, weren't mouthing platitudes. They spoke from experience and trials of their own.

"Their advice is just as true today as it ever was," she pointed out.

At first Hank was skeptical, but as he studied the quotations it dawned on him that they contained the answer to his plight. As a gift, Mary presented him with a handsome leather binder filled with reprints of great sayings that could help him. And she added a little note of her own which read:

"Darling, discouragement is a luxury we can't afford."

Hank took the book with him on his calls and thumbed through it whenever he had a free moment. He developed an optimistic philosophy that routed his depression and got him back on the ball.

He awoke to the fact that the competition weren't supermen and were vulnerable in several respects. He also accepted the notion that no company has a monopoly on excellence. One firm may be weak where another is strong and vice versa. The salesman, he learned, must capitalize on his outfit's virtues and at the same time do his own job so thoroughly and competently that his firm's faults will be submerged by his superb selling techniques.

Hank rose to the top third of his company's sales staff. I last heard he was being recommended for a managerial position with his own sales staff.

Can anyone doubt Euripides' statement that "Man's best possession is a sympathetic wife."

Ways to Fight Discouragement

But there are other ways to combat discouragement. Some salesmen find themselves getting stale after several years on the job. They lose their zest.

When this happens, it might be a good idea to take a vacation or at least ask for a few days off. Go somewhere and forget about selling. Sit under a tree, fish or climb a mountain. Chances are you'll get a new perspective on your job—and yourself.

So many of us rush around without pausing now and then to find out where we are going. A salesman should take time out periodically to have a little chat with himself. The result is often a clearer focus on his ambitions.

Outside activity is another gloom chaser. The salesman who lives 24 hours a day for his job is not being fair to himself, his family or his community. Don't be a one-dimensional man. Find a hobby. Take part in civic affairs. Spend time with your wife and children. This is not only emotionally healthy, but it will give you an opportunity to meet new people, some of whom could be influential to your career.

The sales manager of a front rank auto parts firm insists that his men play some role in the life of their community.

Over lunch one day, he told me:

"Through the years I've found that the men who serve on the school board, head up charity drives or even join the PTA are better salesmen and less apt to be discouraged when the breaks go against them. It's usually the loner, the guy with no outside interest, who lets his problems beat him."

Negativism Ruins Sales

Unless he can hide his feelings, a downhearted salesman can cast a pall over an interview. Radiate confidence and the prospect catches the fever. Show a downcast face and you'll have a short session in his office.

Can you blame the buyer? He's not a father confessor nor a psychiatrist. He's meeting you on a strictly business proposition. He's entitled to a sound, interesting presentation.

If, because of your black mood, your sales talk falls flat, the prospect's reaction might be:

"If he's not enthusiastic about his product, why should I be?"

Buyers are quick to sense lack of morale in a salesman. Such an attitude can be fatal to a sale.

Often the best remedy for those selling blues is to drive straight ahead. Make more calls, do more prospecting, think up new ideas—anything to keep you from wallowing in your own despondency. There's a good chance the problem will unravel itself.

The solution for discouragement will not be the same for all salesmen. Each of us must proceed at his own pace. Inspirational literature may be one man's meat, but indigestible to another. Some men thrive on vacations, while others need only one every five or ten years.

The point I want to hammer home is that no salesman should lie down with his sorrow and make no effort to get up. Man is a thinking animal. Use this gift to lick despair.

Don't turn away from your problem. Face it with fortitude. It isn't any bigger than you are.

29

Not Using the "You" Element in Selling

TOO MANY SALESMEN FAIL TO UNDERSTAND A FUNDA-
mental fact of human nature: a buyer is interested in himself.
If he's in the hardware line, he couldn't care less what your
product did for somebody in the garment business. You can talk
price and quality until you're blue in the face without reaching him. Instead of taking careful aim at a prospect's true interests, some salesmen shoot wildly from the hip and miss the
target.

Recently, I had an opportunity to prepare a case history of
how a salesman muffed a deal just because of such a miscal-
culation. One of my clients, a large electronics firm, planned to
make a big investment in data processing equipment. The
buyer, one of the company's top men, first checked the equipment used by other firms in his field. Then he interviewed
several high-salaried equipment salesmen.

Each week, for six weeks, the buyer gave me a blow-by-blow
account of his interviews with the salesmen. I wish every salesman reading this could have heard him.

"George," my friend said, "I'm astounded at the way these birds talked around the subject. They missed the point all the way down the line."

"How do you mean, Ed?" I asked.

Stay within the Industry

"Well, there was one fellow who really had the product I wanted. I would have done business with him in a minute if he had had sense enough to gear his pitch to my interests. The guy spent two percent of his time on my problems and my business and the other 98 percent on the benefits of his equipment to the banking field. I almost yawned in his face. What do I care about the application of his product to banking? I'm in the electronics business. I wanted to know what his machines will do for us."

Here was an example of one-track thinking. Ed tried several times to get the salesman off the banking rail and onto the main line, but it was a futile effort. The seller lacked imagination, common sense, or both.

A discerning salesman would have realized that my friend was interested chiefly in how his competitors were using the product, and how it was saving them money, time and effort. This fellow was so impressed with the fact that he was making $40,000 a year that he lost sight of the "you" element in selling. This was hip shooting at its wildest! Of course, the man lost the order. Now let's take a look at the salesman who got it.

Know Your Prospect's Problems

"This second fellow," Ed told me, "made a thorough study of our company, our problems and the industry generally. His equipment was not widely used in our business, but this did not deter him for a moment. One day he drove up and suggested we tour the three or four electronics plants using his product to see how they liked it.

"At each firm the salesman got the controllers to do a selling job for him. In one instance, a controller revealed that his company had gotten rid of the other salesman's data processing equipment in favor of the second man's apparatus. This was real selling."

When they got back to Ed's office the salesman really went to work. He cited clear-cut examples of how his equipment could do the same job or better for Ed's firm. And he made out his case with prepared facts and figures.

"I asked him one or two questions and he answered without a bit of hesitation," Ed recalled. "This man had done his homework. He knew what I would be interested in."

The first salesman would have profited greatly if he had seen his competitor in action. The profit would be in the lesson he would have learned.

I am not implying the first man was completely off base. There would have been nothing wrong in occasionally mentioning that the Chase Manhattan bank or the United States Government uses his equipment. But to base an entire sales presentation on such an approach is inviting disaster. The man made the mistake of not meeting the buyer on his home ground, of not coming to grips with him on *his* problems. Instead, the seller tossed in a few big names and naively thought the prospect would be impressed enough to whip out his pen and sign an order. Maybe it had worked before, but this salesman was pushing his luck.

Ed, a highly competent executive, is still rankled by the experience.

"You know, George," he mused, "I would liked to have gone to the president of that other company and told him that I had preferred his product all along but his salesman had dropped the ball."

My friend didn't go because it would have hurt the salesman.

However, there is no question that this $40,000-a-year man flopped miserably. He made the mistake of overlooking the "you" factor in selling. He made the further error of thinking that Ed would commit his firm to an investment running into thousands of dollars merely because a bank used his data processing equipment. An endorsement by ten banks would not have influenced Ed's decision. My friend wanted to know what the product could do for *his* firm.

By now you can see what went wrong. The first salesman simply had not prepared himself to deal with a man of Ed's caliber. The door-to-door gadget salesman may sell his thinga-majig by telling a housewife that Mrs. Jones down the street just bought one. But in a high level situation such tactics won't work. Ed was not buying an egg beater. This was a big business deal. He was putting his reputation with his company right on the line. Ed had been entrusted with great responsibility. Not for a second would he violate that trust by falling for a half-baked sales pitch.

Be Familiar with the Buyer's Needs

The first salesman has probably since learned that shooting out important names and unrelated companies just serves as an appetizer in selling. For the main course, you've got to get down to cases. You must sell the buyer on *his particular needs*. He has the right to know what your product can do for *his* company.

Life insurance salesmen have applied the "you" idea very wisely. They tailor their presentations strictly to the individual. You will never hear a top insurance man telling a prospect that he ought to have a particular kind of policy because Mr. Smith has one. He has figured out the client's policy on the basis of the latter's existing insurance, age, liabilities, dependents, probable income and many other factors. The customer can be assured he is getting an individual "diagnosis."

Of course, life insurance is a more personal kind of selling, but the product salesman can learn much from it. The "you" element is predominant. The insurance seller is attuned to his prospect's individual needs. He does not beat about the bush with irrelevant information.

The broader application of the insurance principle is obvious. The company buyer, too, wants a personal diagnosis. But in this case he wants his firm's particular needs and problems analyzed. If you understand this important fact, you have a key to success as a salesman.

30

Not Using Presentation Aids

A SALESMAN FRIEND OF MINE IS AN AMATEUR MAGICIAN.
One night at a dinner party he performed some slight-of-hand that left us gasping in admiration.

Later, I got him aside and jokingly asked:

"Is that what makes you such a successful salesman, Dick—doing tricks for your customers?"

Dick Palmer, who makes about $50,000 a year selling packaging machinery, suddenly grew serious.

"No, George," he replied, "this is just a hobby, but the principle of what I did tonight can be applied to salesmanship —namely selling by demonstration. After I tell the prospect what my product can do, I *show* him.

"I have display material that enables me to close sales that another two hours of talking could not accomplish."

Dick has avoided a mistake that other salesmen make every day. They don't use valuable tools that have proven themselves time and time again as selling aids.

These tools are familiar to all salesmen. They include exhibits, photographs, models, movies, sound and silent film slides, portfolios, figures, graphs, charts, cartoons, samples, easel pads, blackboards, miniatures and others.

And don't forget that the product itself is an important selling tool. If you've told a buyer that a cigarette lighter will light 100 times out of 100 attempts, pull out the lighter and *show* him. Seeing is believing.

This simple principle is ignored by many salesmen. They scoff at display material as "kid stuff" and let it gather dust in the backs of their cars. You can't even budge them with irrefutable evidence of solid sales made through demonstration.

How mistaken they are! In our mass production economy the difference in products is often superficial. Electric toasters differ only in design; automobiles are unique only in their accessories.

The salesman in a competitive market will fail or succeed on how dramatically and realistically he demonstrates his product. The more vividly he can communicate to the buyer, the more chance he has to make the sale.

But that's showmanship, you say. All right, what's wrong with a little showmanship? Some salesmen and sales managers regard showmanship as a dirty word. How silly! If a man knows his product thoroughly and has confidence in it, showmanship will help him sell it. The salesman is not entertaining the customer with display material. He is showing him the benefits and advantages he has to offer.

Hit the Other Four Senses

We have found that a properly handled portfolio or kit can enhance a presentation tenfold. Man has five senses, of which hearing is only one. If a customer can see, touch, smell or taste the product his resistance becomes easier to crack. In any presentation there is a time to stop talking and start demonstrating.

Sound logic, a resonant voice and a commanding personality certainly improve a presentation, but these qualities are not enough. A buyer's reaction to a 20-minute sales talk may be:

"O.K., you've made your pitch, now lay it on the table. Let's *see* what you've got."

As many salesmen know, a customer's attention span narrows after the first half of a purely oral presentation. This is the law of diminishing return as applied to selling.

Les Kincaid learned the law the hard way. A machine tool salesman, Les suffered an humiliating experience several years ago. A prospect yawned in his face midway through his sales talk.

My friend told me about it the following night while we were bowling.

"I've had it," Les complained bitterly. "I'm getting out of selling. That was a terrible blow and I don't want to get hurt that way again."

"Before you quit," I said, "I'd like you to come with me to a PTA meeting tomorrow night."

Les was dumbfounded. "A PTA meeting!" he exclaimed. "I'm not even a member."

"That's all right," I assured him. "Come anyway."

He agreed.

We arrived as a representative for a charitable organization was launching an appeal for donations to send underprivileged youngsters to summer camp. His speech was standard stuff that left the audience restive and somewhat bored.

Then the room was darkened for movies. The film showed the kids at camp They were having a wonderful time swimming, playing volleyball and gobbling up huge platefuls of food. Their scrawny bodies told more vividly than words ever could of their deprivation.

When the lights went on virtually every person there gave or pledged money.

I had known about the fund drive and as we were leaving I said to Les:

"You saw the answer tonight to your problem. Perhaps only

three people in 10 would have shelled out on the basis of the speech alone. But when they saw those kids they were sold—in their hearts and in their minds. It was more than an emotional appeal. The audience *saw* the good their money would do."

Les looked perplexed. "But what does this have to do with my selling?" he asked.

"Everything," I retorted. "You have good visual aids you're not using. After you tell the prospect about your product, show him. Bring out the tools your company provided to emphasize your message. The buyer wants more than promises; he wants proof."

Les took my advice and in a year he tripled his profits. He's now district manager with a crew of 35 salesmen. He not only urges them to use demonstration material, but he also demands it. He convinced one skeptic by accompanying the man to the customer's office and putting on the show himself. The skeptic became a believer when the prospect doubled his previous order.

Be Sure Everything Works

Demonstrations need not always follow the sales talk. Sometimes it's better to open the interview with color slides or charts as an attention hook. Then, after a short explanation, a more complete visual presentation can be staged to clinch the sale.

However, the most elaborate equipment in the world is useless in inept hands. A salesman should plan and rehearse his performance so he won't bungle the main event. He must decide what to demonstrate and in what order. He should time his presentation to avoid snags and delays that will exasperate the purchaser. He should make sure everything works. Screens that don't unwind, slides in the wrong order and easels that don't stand up can turn the demonstration into an embarrassing nightmare.

A smart salesman will practice at home until he can run through the presentation smoothly and expertly and knows his material cold. Let your wife be the buyer and tell her not to pull any punches in criticizing your performance.

Display material has been thoroughly researched and tested before the salesman ever gets it. So he benefits from the knowledge and know-how of promotion and advertising experts who have made a career of motivating buyers. The man who complains that he doesn't have time to sell because he's overloaded with display material is missing the whole point. Demonstrating *is* selling.

Some salesmen are afraid to set up their displays in the prospect's office. Their fear is groundless. Our studies have shown that buyers like demonstrations. Their interest in the product shoots up when they see it in action. Well-managed displays are fast-moving, provocative and easy to understand. The prospect's opposition is broken down when he can see an item's merits in graphic form. A single chart or slide can do more to drive home the message than an hour's monologue. Moreover, it's easier for the buyer to refer back to the graph or photo to remember everything the salesman has said.

Everybody Should Get Into the Act

A good idea is to let the customer handle the display or product himself. Make him part of the act. He learns firsthand what the product will do.

Creating desire is one of the seller's most important tasks. What better way to accomplish this than by live, exciting demonstrations?

It's a mistake not to use display material, but it's equally wrong to rely on the demonstration alone to carry the day. Some salesmen are so impressed with their kits and folders that they let them do all the work. Their only contribution is to periodically flip over a chart or insert a slide into a machine. As one sales manager put it to me:

"The guy becomes an automaton. He's so hypnotized by what he's showing that he forgets to talk."

An intelligent, well-organized sales talk should be built around the demonstration. While the salesman is showing he should be talking. The amount of wordage depends on the type of display. There's no sense in repeating what the buyer can see for himself. This only insults his intelligence.

But the right word at the right time effectively interprets the demonstration and plugs up any gaps in the display material. Talking also covers up any awkward pauses while arranging or moving equipment.

The wise salesman will find out as much as he can about the prospect before the demonstration. Thus, the displays can be tailored to the prospect's special needs and the salesman is prepared to field any questions thrown at him.

Accentuate the Positive

Product demonstration is an effective selling weapon. If a salesman is sincere and truthful about his merchandise there's nothing wrong with using showmanship as part of his proposition.

If you guarantee a leak-proof paper carton, fill it with water and let the buyer see for himself what you mean. If ease and speed of assembly is one of your selling points, toss the parts on the prospect's desk and fit them together. Do you stress the durability of your product? Bang it with a mallet a few times.

Such demonstrations should make a definite point. Mere razzle-dazzle will not get your show off the ground. The buyer can go to a nightclub or watch television if he wants only entertainment. In short, demonstrate the product—not yourself.

My friend, Dick Palmer, would never dream of trying to sell a prospect by means of the hocus-pocus with which he amuses his friends. His sales demonstrations are based on the principles of sound reasoning and good taste. The buyer is not tricked; he is given a clear-cut display of how the packaging machinery will help his business.

A theatrical press agent once brought a trained seal into a newspaper office. The seal had nothing to do with the show the man was publicizing. The mammal was just an attention getter. Both were tossed out by a city editor who had no time for such foolishness.

The moral of the story is that the salesman should not exhaust the buyer's time and patience with pointless hoopla. But the salesman must have genuine enthusiasm for his product and the display. The best audio-visual equipment in the world is wasted if the man behind it is listless and apathetic. Demonstration paraphernalia is a selling tool. It cannot, by itself, produce the desired results. Television is a fascinating medium but no commercial announcer relies solely on the wonder of airborne pictures to sell the product. These salesmen describe their wares with conviction and spirit. To test the importance of the announcer's role, switch off the audio during a commercial. Notice how flat and lifeless the picture is.

Display apparatus won't make a good salesman out of a poor one. It won't cover up his lack of knowledge about the product. It won't supply his enthusiasm.

But in the hands of a capable, enthusiastic and knowledgeable salesman, such material will make selling more profitable, more professional and more interesting.

31

Being Liked But Not Respected

WE ALL WANT TO BE LIKED. IT'S A HUMAN DESIRE.
Salesmen are no exception to this feeling, but the man who
makes a career of being liked is making a mistake. It's more
important that he be respected.

The salesman who is respected will usually find that he is
also liked. The two qualities are natural partners.

Let me give you an illustration. Marty Saunders, a newcomer
to selling, was assigned to call on top management people for
a prominent business service firm. By nature, he was not a
back-slapping, jovial individual. A college math and engineering major, he was more inclined to be introspective, even
slightly introverted. So Marty approached his new job with
some misgivings. He had always heard that salesmen are outgoing, *bon vivant* types, who got orders by charming prospects.

"That kind of approach is not for me and I know it," he
told his wife, Laura, before his first call. "I can't change my
nature and I'm not sure I should."

Instead, he did some deep thinking about the task ahead.

He reasoned that, if 100 salesmen in any industry are calling
on a prospect, there are 100 producers of that product. The

probability in this case would be that a particular buyer would purchase from no more than five percent of these sellers.

"If they're all likeable guys," he told Laura, "it's obvious that the five percent making the sales must have something else working for them. And if the other 95 percent are trying to make it on personality alone, they're wasting their time."

Marty decided that the way to join the five percent group was to get himself respected by prospects. He, of course, would be friendly, but in addition, he would strive to earn a reputation for honesty, integrity, and dependability. If those qualities made him liked—fine.

The idea, novel in Marty's territory, was an immediate success. His conduct was so high-principled that prospects automatically associated his product and company with quality.

Buyers began to realize that Marty stood behind his word. He never made exaggerated claims nor ran down the competition. He was loyal to both his house and the customer, whose interests he looked after. At the same time, he permitted neither his company nor the buyer to get away with anything. Even his business correspondence reflected his strict code of honor.

In keeping with his general behavior, Marty wore quiet clothing in good taste, was punctual in keeping appointments, and never wasted the prospect's time with irrelevant chatter.

Marty's earning rose so rapidly for a freshman salesman that he earned more bonuses than some veterans who had been with the organization 15 and 20 years

Respect, Not Friendship, Makes the Sale

This young man learned an important fact of life: Buyers want to do business with salesmen and firms they can respect. Friendships are all right, but prospects would rather reserve their camaraderie for the club locker room. Between nine and five they're running a business and expect the salesmen to react accordingly.

Many salesmen make such a fetish of being liked that they frequently leave a prospect's office with a handshake instead of an order. It has been a perfectly pleasant visit, but with no payoff.

If such a salesman is at all discerning, he will notice in time that the purchaser has adopted a kind of patronizing attitude toward him. The buyer considers him a pleasant fellow, but not the sort of person to whom he wants to give his business. Both the salesman and his product are characterized as lacking substance.

Even worse, this type of relationship can reach the point where the salesman is simply regarded as amusing and nothing else. The old adage that "familiarity breeds contempt" bears strongly on salesmanship.

Don't Overdo the Glad Hand Approach

I'm not suggesting that a salesman alter his personality so that he becomes stern, humorless, and even dull. What I am proposing is that he not swing completely the other way to become a caricature of a toothpaste ad, hoping to attract orders by his dazzling smile and hearty manner. In this highly competitive economy it takes more than personality to make a good living.

It's the salesmen like Marty Saunders who carry home the big prizes. These individuals have achieved a proper balance between friendliness and respect. They know that it helps them to be different. They don't run with the pack.

When I was a young salesman, a veteran of years on the road gave me some advice I never forgot.

"George," he counseled. "Never be afraid to stand up for what you think is right. Once in a while you may rub a prospect the wrong way, but in the long run you'll earn the admiration of everyone you come in contact with. You can be a successful salesman without being a doormat."

I had occasion years later to pass on this advice to a bright young man working for a client firm.

This fellow, Clay Harris, had been hired right out of college, where he had been a highly successful campus politician. He was president of his fraternity in his junior year and the following year he was elected president of the entire student body.

The qualities which brought him these honors included good looks, an engaging smile, impeccable manners, and a bouncing enthusiasm for any cause he embraced.

Clay's firm, which manufactured asbestos products, assigned him to a northeastern territory where the competition already held the edge.

He worked hard and lost no time in getting himself known. But orders trickled in so slowly that his employer began to wonder if he had made the right choice. His competitors not only continued to hold the edge, but increased it.

"I can't understand it," Clay lamented to me one day. "I think the prospects like me and I knock myself out trying to please them. Yet I just can't seem to score where it counts."

He was quite distraught and to calm him down I asked him to describe his approach and conduct with prospects in more detail. As he narrated his experiences, I could see at once where the trouble lay.

"Clay," I told him, "you're trying too hard to be a nice guy. I know about your college background, but to get along in this business you've got to be something more than an all-American boy. Prospects and customers appreciate the qualities which made you shine in college, but they aren't enough."

I then explained the importance of commanding respect to set him apart from the crowd.

"Thousands of salesmen are trying to get by on personality alone," I continued. "It's the man who isn't afraid to be different who succeeds. If your conscience and good judgment tell you that you should say 'no,' then do it. The momentary annoyance it may cause someone will be nothing compared to the reputation you'll eventually build for yourself."

Clay put this idea into practice with wonderful results. Far from dropping in the esteem of his prospects, he actually placed himself on a friendlier footing with them. Buyers not only swore by his character and word, but they clamored for his social companionship. He had invitations to dinner from almost all his customers, who thought of him as a good friend.

The point of this story is that the salesman need not sacrifice his "nice guy" qualities to be respected by his prospects and customers. The chances are that he'll be liked even more—and at the same time maintain his self-respect.

The men who scaled the heights of the business world didn't do so by winning popularity contests among their associates and customers. They thought it more important to be respected than merely liked. The individuals who concentrated solely on being liked wound up at lower or middle management and stayed there.

Cultivating habits which earn esteem often require courage. It's always easier to go along with the herd. One feels safe and protected. But somewhere along the line you've got to break out of the mold. I assure you it will be worthwhile. One day a prospect will hold his hand out to you and say:

"You are a man I respect."

Can you think of a higher compliment?

32

Selling Technology Instead of Benefits

ONE OF THE BEST SALESMEN I HAVE EVER KNOWN WAS AN 18-year-old boy who worked in a gas station near my home.

Eddie believed there was more to his job than pumping gas or changing tires. He really tried to sell products his employer carried.

One day I drove in for an oil change which Eddie usually handled for me.

"Mr. Kahn," he said, "we have a new oil you ought to try."

"But I'm satisfied with the oil I've been using," I replied.

Eddie then gave me a flawless, five-minute sales talk on the new product. His presentation was built around what his brand of oil would do for my car, and how it was really made for an automobile like mine. He explained that this particular oil was necessary for my high-powered motor. In other words, he talked benefits to me.

I bought the oil (which cost a little more, incidentally) and found Eddie had been giving me the straight dope. Even my dealer agreed with the boy.

Eddie also recommended other products, always putting the emphasis on how they would improve my car's performance or extend its life. He talked very little about the technical aspects of the item, whether it was a windshield wiper or a radiator flushing compound.

That lad illustrated a priceless ingredient in selling—reaching the buyer on a personal level.

Technical Terms Can Lose You Sales

Countless salesmen make the mistake of not relating the product to the buyer's needs. They swamp the prospect with technical terms that are not meaningful to him. Usually, this type of salesman is a walking encyclopedia of facts about his line. He knows every component that goes into the product, which he can trace back to the first prototype. All this is very well, but it doesn't move merchandise. The prospect doesn't want a short course in engineering. He is seeking the application of the product to his own situation.

A man who learned this after painful experience was Keith Banning, who started his career in the production department of a big appliance manufacturer.

It had always been Keith's idea to switch to selling and one day his opportunity came. The personnel manager said there was a vacancy in the northeastern territory which Keith could have.

The young man jumped at the chance and tackled the job with enthusiasm and determination. In one respect, Keith was well qualified for selling. Thanks to his company's policy of giving employees experience in all operations, he had learned a tremendous amount about its products and knew them in minutest detail. He also was 100 percent convinced they were the finest of their kind on the market.

Well, Keith sailed into his interviews like a kind of Messiah carrying the word to the buyer. He rattled off so much detail and technical jargon that prospects sought desperately for an excuse to get rid of him.

Keith also bored in hard with a long account of the production process that was equally meaningless to the listener.

Buyer Is Seldom Production-Oriented

What Keith failed to consider was that those purchasing agents were not production-oriented. They were not interested in manufacturing techniques, or in mechanical details. In their mind, the competition offered basically the same product, and, in addition, had created consumer demand which the buyer could parlay into sales.

Keith felt his product was superior to the competition's, but he made no headway with buyers because he didn't talk their language. People act in their own interests. The salesman who hits the top brackets speaks to the prospect in terms of profits, savings, comfort, safety, convenience, prestige, popularity, and economy. The intricacies of the manufacturing process play no part in buying motives.

Keith's sales manager, Larry Abbott, explained about buyers' motivation to him.

"Look," he told the discouraged salesman, "your knowledge of the industrial process is fine if you can relate it to the buyer's interest."

"How do you mean?" Keith asked.

"Well," his chief replied, "we ran surveys, for example, that showed we only have two breakdowns for every 1,000 toasters we sell. Our competitors have from three to twelve times that many. Giving the buyer only the cold figures won't get you far. But you can stimulate his desire by telling him how important such facts are to his profits and customer relationships. When an appliance breaks down, he risks not only losing a customer, but also many other customers who will hear that the store sells a bad product.

"This will cause them to be suspicious of other items in the place. Besides, he must think of the time and cost of adjusting the broken toaster."

Keith got the message. He began approaching buyers in terms of the customer loyalty and confidence that his products would inspire.

"It's like this," he told one prospect. "A customer who gets stuck with a faulty appliance may boycott 75 other departments in your store. It might be a good idea to bring this factor up at your merchandising meetings."

The buyer thought it was an excellent suggestion and carried it out that same week. He invited Keith in to talk to the group. With his expert knowledge of production and research, Keith was able to demonstrate to managers that his product could save them money and improve their image.

Relate Technology to Customer Benefits

At the same time, Keith pointed out how quality control procedures by his company reduced customer irritation with appliances that won't work. He invited buyers to visit the plant to see for themselves the production line techniques. When quality control was related to loss of customers, prospects perked up and listened. This was no dry harangue or technical mumbo-jumbo.

When one dealer remonstrated that his store had extremely few complaints, Keith had a ready answer. A survey sponsored by his firm revealed that most shoppers, women particularly, don't return and raise heck about a faulty product. They simply take their business elsewhere. Still not convinced, the dealer made his own survey and got the same results. From then on, he regarded Keith as a kind of infallible oracle.

The salesman must impress on the buyer that although he receives merchandise in carloads, the product is sold individually to one customer at a time. Like a shock wave, a bad unit can spread consumer dissatisfaction to the point where it takes in the entire store, not only the department in which the purchase was made.

This kind of information makes sense to the prospect. The salesman should think like a buyer if he is to win the latter's attention and confidence.

A good salesman first learns his product thoroughly with an eye to the benefits, advantages and satisfactions it holds for the potential customer. He studies each buyer, determining his desires and motivations

Only then can the salesman drive nome his message. He can use his expert knowledge of the company's research and production to satisfy buyer needs and calm his worries and fears. He puts himself in the buyer's shoes and tries to imagine what features of a presentation would most appeal to him.

After all, the buyer or prospect places a high value on peace of mind. He wants to know that he is getting a reliable product that will not only move well, but will also not cause him worry or concern in the form of complaints from customers. Nothing can make a buyer angrier than undependable products. Items that break down or fail to deliver what they promise cost a dealer much in loss of prestige and sales. The salesman who assures him that will not happen is bound to get an attentive ear.

No salesman can expect to anticipate every need or problem of the buyer. But if he trains himself to think of his product in terms of what it can do for the buyer, he is thinking along correct lines and is headed for success.

Take Advantage of Your Product's Assets

The idea of relating the product to the buyer and his customer reminds me of Link Evans, who sells athletic equipment to schools and colleges. The factor Link stresses above all is safety. He knows schools do everything possible to prevent sports injuries. When a youngster is hurt or killed on the playing field it not only affects the parents, but the school, the community, the boy's teammates and others. There is also the question of the school's liability in such accidents. These are some of the reasons behind the many precautions taken to prevent injuries and deaths.

So when Link is giving a sales talk to a coach or athletic director he tells the product story in terms of what it will do to hold down or eliminate the danger of injuries. If the item is a football headpiece, his main pitch will be on the research that has gone into the helmet to cut down face and head injuries. A similar assurance is given in selling tumbling mats and other gymnasium equipment.

Link would consider it the height of absurdity to relate the product story in terms of the durability of the plastic, the stuffing in the mats, etc., without tying it in with safety. The coach will not be much impressed if he learns that the plastic helmet has been subjected to a certain chemical process. But if he can be shown that the headgear will offer sure-fire protection, he will react positively.

Another factor close to the heart of school buyers is economy. Athletic departments don't have unlimited budgets, as Link well knows. So he stresses toughness of basketball nets and other equipment in terms of longevity. He has seen the result of lab tests made with the nets and can tell a buyer they will stand up under months of heavy use. This is talking the buyer's language.

You can see how superior this is to dwelling on such dreary facts as the number of fibers in the netting or the amount of foam in the shoulder pads.

Tell the sales story in the language the buyer can understand and relate to his own needs. Establish empathy with the buyer or prospect. To speak only in technical terminology is sterile and defeating. If you are technical, be technical with a purpose.

Remember, you are selling benefits, not technology.

33

Not Seeing Yourself Objectively

WE ARE ALL A LITTLE NEARSIGHTED WHEN WE LOOK AT ourselves.

We may not be sure about the impression we make on others, but we know how we look to ourselves—in an admirable light, of course. In other words, we tend to overlook our faults and magnify our virtues.

Most of the time there is little harm in such deception and conceit, but for a salesman it can be expensive. He must see himself as others do if he is to advance in his career.

The salesman is on exhibit every day of his working life. He is appraised by his superiors, his colleagues and most important, his prospects and customers. The wrong word, a boorish action, even a tasteless tie could doom a $100,000 order.

I knew a salesman who once dropped a big sale because he lit a cigarette in the prospect's office. The fact that there were no ashtrays should have tipped him off, but he simply flicked the ashes into the waste basket. The buyer could not stand cigarette smoke, but was too polite to tell the salesman. He made his displeasure known by withholding an order he had been prepared to give.

Periodic Appraisal Is Necessary

Self-analysis would have prevented such a blunder. Periodically, the salesman must stand away from himself, as it were, and see himself as he impresses other people. He must be conscious of appearance, dress and manner wherever he goes. Even during social activities he should comport himself as a gentleman.

The human personality is the end product of many years of development. It is impossible to change the habits of a lifetime overnight, but we can take inventory of ourselves to determine our weak and strong points. Then we can modify our behavior, dress or manner to make ourselves more likable and thus lay the foundation for future success. But it takes honesty and effort.

I have known many salesmen whose habits or characteristics were definitely hurting them on the job. Yet virtually all of these drawbacks could have been corrected with sufficient effort and determination. When the man made no move to improve himself it was usually because he did not have the self-honesty to admit that he was not 100 percent perfect. And he was resentful when somebody tried to destroy this illusion for his own good. I can testify to this from personal experience.

Four Traits Needed to Be Liked

Psychological research has shown that there are four traits most frequently mentioned by men as accounting for liking another man.

They are intelligence, cheerfulness, friendliness and congeniality of interests. Intelligence is the only one of these that can't be improved through application. But I will assume that if you are a salesman, you must be pretty well endowed with intelligence. This is no business for the feeble-minded.

The other three traits then should not be a problem. You can train yourself to be more cheerful, to act friendlier and to develop interests which fit in with those of your prospects and customers. At least you can take time to learn enough about the other fellow's interests to talk about them.

My years in selling have taught me this basic truth: If you start out by liking people, they will usually respond by liking you. But there is more to making a good impression than that. The problem of many salesmen is that they are unaware of certain characteristics which make them obnoxious to other people.

Take a Chance and Ask Your Friends

One of my friends, Fred Lawrence, was one of these salesmen. He was, however, different in one respect: He knew something was wrong in his make-up, but he could not put his finger on it. Then he got an idea. It took plenty of guts to put the idea into operation, but it helped him overcome his handicaps.

He asked several of his friends and customers to list on an unsigned piece of paper the traits which they admired most and least in him. Some of the answers gave Fred quite a jolt—but in the right direction. He began working on his bad points and soon had them mastered.

"It was quite a revelation," Fred admitted to me. "I did not realize that I spent too much time talking and not enough listening. I also was unaware that I had an annoying habit of interrupting others while they were talking."

Fred added that anyone he knew would have done him a great favor by pointing out these failings to him. But this rarely happens. Because of not wanting to hurt a person's feelings these things go unsaid. The advertisement about body odor is pretty true to life. "Her Best Friends Wouldn't Tell Her," was a realistic bit of copywriting.

Substitute Good Habits for Bad Ones

One way to shed a bad habit is to substitute a good one for it. Perhaps you can't toss off the bad habit entirely, but you can do something to offset it. For example, if you blow your own horn too much, try and get in a plug now and then for the people who back you up—your sales manager, production people, etc.

You also might say a kind word about the prospect or his firm, without laying it on too heavily. Show that you have some interest outside yourself.

After you have pinpointed your bad habits you can't just let it go at that. You must use the new habit at every opportunity. If your trouble is that you don't smile enough, make it a point to smile whether you feel like it or not. The practice will help.

Whatever happens, don't let yourself fall back into your old ways once the improvement process takes hold. Otherwise, you'll be right back where you started.

The kind of a salesman you are depends a lot on the kind of person you are. If you are warm-hearted, unselfish and outgoing, these qualities will reflect themselves in the way you handle your job. This is true of other professions as well since most people are selling something in life. The clergyman, teacher, doctor, politician are, in a sense, all salesmen. A boy courting a girl is a salesman.

Confidence Is Needed

Another quality which a salesman needs is confidence—in himself and his product. Lack of confidence will cause a salesman to freeze up when confronting a prospect. His presentation is halting, dull and disorganized.

The fault here is that the salesman does not recognize one

of the simplest rules of salesmanship: More than half the battle is won if the salesman has something worthwhile that the prospect needs. If he can then make the buyer feel this need and recognize the worth of his product, the battle is his.

The salesman should also concentrate on getting the prospect interested in himself. You can make yourself the kind of person who will attract and hold the prospect's attention.

The salesman who recognizes only his virtues while ignoring his faults may achieve the heights in self-esteem but he will never be a successful seller.

I can best illustrate this by telling a story of two young men who started together in selling about 15 years ago. Jack Norris and Dave Sanders were recruited from a midwestern college by a leading paint manufacturer.

Although the two were good friends, they had completely different philosophies concerning their jobs.

"At five o'clock," Jack said, "I'm through and forget all about business until the next day. If I have paperwork I do it, but that's all."

Dave, on the other hand, never stopped thinking about his work and ways to improve himself. And he didn't have to be a drudge to accomplish this. He used part of his free time to evaluate himself. He would run through in his mind his performances that day and try and find weaknesses. He also tried to imagine how he impressed various prospects. He practiced before mirrors to control his facial expressions. He rehearsed sales talks before his wife. When he spotted a weakness he worked on it until it was eliminated.

In five years Dave's income tripled while Jack slogged along without making any progress. Finally, Jack asked Dave to help him.

"What's wrong with me?" he asked.

"You are too complacent," Dave told him frankly. "You think that a college education and wearing the right clothes are enough to get you by. In themselves they're fine, but you must work harder at being a good salesman. You must spend some time in self-improvement."

"I don't want to spend 24 hours a day on selling," Jack protested. "There are other things in life."

"Of course there are," Dave agreed, "and you can enjoy them even more if you become a better salesman. You may be surprised to learn that I spend only an hour each evening trying to correct my mistakes."

The difference was that Dave had the insight to look at himself objectively—harshly if necessary. Jack did not want to examine himself too closely for fear of what he would find.

But eventually Jack got the idea and did a lot of homework in the next few months. He stepped aside, so to speak, and took a realistic look at himself for the first time. The experience was rewarding for he is now one of the top earners in the company.

Don't be afraid of self-appraisal and self-criticism. These are tools by which you can mature and grow as a salesman. There is no such thing as a born success. The top producers today earned their status. Each one of them at some stage in his career took a hard look at himself and decided to make some changes.

Hold the mirror up and do the same.

34

Ignoring Good Will

WHAT IS GOOD WILL, YOU MAY ASK?

Well, it is not created by an occasional slap on the back or by telling jokes. The old-time drummer may have thrived on such tactics but today's tough competition demands a far more intelligent approach, and unless the salesman is selling houses, yachts, or some other once-in-a-lifetime item, his income depends, in large part, on repeat orders. Yet many men act as if their first call will be their last, doing little or nothing to win the prospect's good will and confidence. This may be all right for a sidewalk pitchman selling windup toys but not for the individual who wants success and security.

A Many-Faceted Foundation

Good will, then, is hammered out of many things—satisfying complaints, handling orders promptly, helping the customer move the product, being on the level, telling the product story convincingly, attractive presentation, consideration for the purchaser's time and feeling, and many more.

Dan Harley, a topnotch sales manager with deep insight,

summed up the good will factor beautifully in a story he told me at lunch one day.

One of his salesmen, Fred Lang, came to him one afternoon, tired and discouraged.

"I don't know what's wrong, but I just can't seem to beat out the competition in my territory," he lamented.

Dan came right to the point.

'If you want sympathy," he said, "I can give it to you by the bucket. But sympathy won't buy your groceries so I'm going to bawl you out instead.

"The company is spending thousands of dollars for advertising, promotion and public relations which could be working for you. Yet you ignore these aids completely. You won't even take the trouble to look over this material."

"Advertising and promotion isn't in my department," Fred protested.

"That's where you're wrong," Dan countered. "Our consumer promotion efforts and media advertising can mean money in your pocket. These activities arouse interest in the product but it's up to the salesman to capitalize on this interest, to follow through on the advertising and publicity campaigns. They should be used to beef up the presentation."

Dan finally convinced Fred that there was a big hole in his selling that needed plugging. The salesman had taken the company's advertising and promotion for granted without relating them to his own job. He was blind to the good will potential in these activities.

Fred started working on his weakness. He gathered up all his firm's advertising and promotional material for the past three years and waded through it over the weekend. He did the same with his competitor's ads and promotional claims, carefully comparing the two and making notes. The research provided him with valuable information for his sales talk.

He also took ad tear sheets and reproductions on his calls

and showed them to his customers. The copies helped Fred close sales that otherwise would have been lost.

In six months his earnings doubled and he is now one of his firm's best money-makers.

Good Will in Company's Services

Salesmen like Fred also overlook other benefits their companies offer customers, such as research facilities, laboratory testing, display material and cost control systems. These services create good will for the salesman who brings them to the prospect's attention. A dealer in Grand Island, Nebraska or Medicine Bow, Wyoming can't be expected to know about these services unless the salesman tells him. Some firms make it easy for the salesman to acquire this information but often he must dig it out himself.

Good Will in Helping the Customer to Sell

Anything a salesman can do for the customer beyond taking his order helps build good will.

A good example is Sam Hall, a pesticide salesman who has made himself an expert on retailing. He stimulates dealers to make their stores more attractive and then shows them how to do it. The payoff is in increased profits and good will from customers who consider him a friend and an authority on merchandising, which he is.

There's an interesting and revealing story behind Sam's accomplishment.

When he was first married, he and his wife bought a combination clothes washer and dryer from an appliance dealer in their small suburban community. After making the down payment, Sam happened to see the newspaper ad of a discount house that was selling the same unit for less money. He could have kicked himself. The young couple was living on a small budget and the savings would have been welcome.

The machine arrived a few days later and with it the dealer who personally supervised the installation and wiring by his men. He then proceeded to give Sam's wife several useful tips on how to extend the automatic's life, cut down repair bills and get better service. He advised her, for example, that very hot water was unnecessary and warned her that prolonged operation wore down parts. He even suggested a soap that produced the cleanest clothes, according to independent tests.

Finally, the appliance dealer demonstrated the unit himself by washing and drying a load of Sam's dirty shirts. He stayed until the Halls were completely satisfied with the machine.

Everything the man said proved true. The Hall's machine outlasted most of their neighbors' washer-dryers and maintenance costs were much lower.

That dealer taught Sam a lesson he never forgot. The owner created good will and confidence by giving the customer extra service and attention that helped him get the maximum benefit from the appliance. He put himself in the buyer's shoes by anticipating the latter's problems with the product.

Sam, for whom building good will was a deficiency, lost no time in putting the lesson into practice in his territory. He studied dozens of books on retail selling, store operation, planning and design, point of sale techniques, customer relations and even interior decorating. He also enrolled in a night course in retail policies and practices despite the fact that he was dead tired after a day's work.

In time Sam knew more about retailing than most of his customers and could have successfully taken over any store in his district.

Today, at least five other companies are bidding for him and he is the highest earner in his line.

Daily experiences and observations offer the salesman many opportunities to patch up his weak spots and advance his career. Inspiration may come from sports, education, business and politics.

Learn from a Politician

The governor of a midwestern state, elected and re-elected four times, developed a phenomenal memory for names, faces and personal facts about his constituents. He could shake the hand of a farmer in a remote village and ask him how his boy, Ralph, was getting along at the state university or whether his hogs won first prize at the county fair as they did the year before.

Now this politician didn't absorb this data through osmosis. He trained himself to remember these facts and aided the process by omnivorous reading. He could skim through 50 newspapers a day. In addition, he kept files on thousands of voters.

When the governor was a young lawyer he had trouble remembering the names of acquaintances. He simply worked on this failing until he beat it.

The salesman can do the same with his weakness. To some selling is an art; others call it a science. Whatever you term it, it's a job that demands the best of a man. He should be prepared to pour into it all the skill, energy and intelligence he has.

The successful salesman is one who has identified his weakness, sought and found a solution and eventually mastered it through self-discipline and hard work.

35

Matching Price Instead of Selling Quality

SOONER OR LATER, EVERY SALESMAN GETS CAUGHT IN A
price squeeze.

Competitors offer what appears to be the same product for
less money, and snatch away business. The affected salesman
can either throw up his hands in disgust, or he can take positive
action to combat this demoralizing situation.

Andy Moss, faced with this predicament, took direct action
and won the day for himself and his company. A synthetic dyes
salesman, Andy was given a tough territory, notorious for its
no-holds-barred type of competition. It took him only three
days on the job to understand what his sales manager meant
when he said, "This will be a challenge to you."

Intensely bitter competition had produced a downward price
spiral that ripped profits to shreds. Most of the companies
handling that product line were barely breaking even and
some were losing money.

At first, Andy was angry and confused. He knew he worked

for a high caliber firm that had been in business for many years, and had a fair price policy.

He reached his lowest point one day when a purchasing agent gently said to him:

"Andy, I like you, but I can get the same stuff you're selling for 20 percent less. I'm going to have to give the business to your competitor."

Andy was intelligent and didn't push the matter then. But, he was alarmed enough to ask his company's treasurer for help.

The treasurer was as upset as Andy. He sat down with the salesman and went carefully over the cost of the product from raw material procurement to final production, including direct and indirect labor costs, overhead, advertising, promotion, and so forth. The officials convinced Andy that the firm was lucky if it netted three or four percent profit after taxes.

"We just can't do it any other way," he explained to Andy. "For the life of me, I cannot understand how our competitors can sell for 20 percent less than we do."

Andy knew the treasurer was giving him straight dope. On the other hand, he also respected the dealer's word and didn't want to argue with him.

"Why not let me show these figures to the prospect?" Andy suggested.

The treasurer refused, as a matter of company policy.

It appeared that Andy was up against a stone wall, but he was not the type to give up easily. He began a one-man research project that provided his solution.

By checking with his industry's association, Dun & Bradstreet, and the Department of Commerce, he uncovered the surprising information that his competitors' costs were the same as his firm's.

There were about 250 companies in the industry, and all paid the same for raw material, labor, maintenance, depreciation, etc. The figures showed that the average firm wound up with a two to four per cent net profit after taxes.

Andy returned to the purchasing agent and laid it on the line.

There's a Joker in the Deck

"Look, Mr. Brown," he said, "something is all wrong here. I can't give you our production costs, but I can tell you that every other outfit in the trade is faced with the same costs and ends up with an average profit. It's my belief that if someone has offered you the same product for 20 percent less, there's a joker in it someplace, and you should recognize it. The difference must be sliced out of raw material, labor or sales costs. The opposition isn't in business to dole out charity. That 20 per-cent margin must be accounted for."

"That may be true," the buyer replied, "but what has this to do with me? I'm getting the product for less, and that's all I care about."

The discussion ended in a standoff, but Andy felt he had left the agent with something to chew over.

In subsequent calls on the same prospect, Andy played the same tune, with different lyrics. He covered every aspect of the industry's costs, but never mentioned those of his company. And he always left the impression that there was something fishy about that 20 per cent "discount."

Andy always backed his claim with strong statistical data.

One day the agent brushed aside Andy's figures and said: "Never mind, I'm satisfied."

He then gave him one of the largest orders he or his firm had ever received. Andy was naturally pleased, but he also was curious, and asked the man for an explanation.

"You said there was a joker in your competitor's low price, and you were right," the agent retorted. "We learned this out-fit has been offering the same price to others around the country and everybody who bought got burned, including ourselves. Their deliveries were late, the quality of their product fell way below standard. Further, the company is in dire financial straits, because of its pricing policy."

The agent said that his organization, which orders six to eight months ahead, had been left holding the bag on a tight schedule for a new product. The shipment arrived late, causing the firm financial hardship and loss of prestige with its customers.

Andy didn't want to rub it in, but he might have said to that agent:

"You never get anything for nothing. If you buy quality and dependability, you have to pay for it."

Don't Ask for Price Cuts, Sell Better

In a price spiral, many salesmen feel they have to "fight fire with fire." The trouble is that they use the wrong kind of fire. They run back to their employer, crying "foul" and asking for permission to sell at the competitor's price. They don't pause to realize that, although price is important today, there are many selling arguments to mount against it—reliability, quality, on-time delivery, research facilities, merchandising help, promotion and many others.

Everyone tries to keep costs down, but most purchasers will pay a higher price for quality and service. If this were not true, the market would be monopolized by cheap, skimpy products. A firm anxious to protect a reputation built up over many years will think twice about risking that name by palming off substandard merchandise and using poor equipment.

Rather than let an interview center entirely around price, the salesman should accent quality, special benefits to customers, service and company reputation. He should also exude an air of quality himself.

In a popular novel of a few years ago, the unemployed hero was seeking a top position with a prominent advertising agency. Before his interview with the head of the outfit, he stopped at an expensive haberdasher and bought a $35 tie, although he had $50 to his name. The man wanted to impress the ad exec, and he did. In fact, the latter complimented him on the tie, which went well with his $175 suit and $60 shoes. The hero was selling himself, and did it by presenting an appearance of confident prosperity, rather than that of a down-at-the-heels supplicant.

By his dress, appearance and even his briefcase, the salesman, with quality to sell, should himself be a walking example of that quality. The big producer is more than an errand boy for his territory. He is an all-around specialist who is attuned to his prospect's needs and problems. Instead of engaging in futile discussions about competitive prices, the smart salesman talks about security the buyer can enjoy in dealing with his company. He stresses its reputation, reliability and record of good service.

You Sacrifice Something When You Cut Price

Anybody can cut prices if he is willing to sacrifice something else. After making this clear to the purchaser, the salesman should move on to the factors which make his product a better buy, *regardless of price*.

Whit Lambert, a corrugated box salesman, stuck to this principle even when it seemed a hopeless extravagance in a market that was more intrigued by price than quality.

His firm thought so much of the quality of its product that it ran continuous tests to insure that customer needs would always be met. Indeed, the company was often ahead of the buyer in this respect. Whit drove this fact home on every call. As a result, he created a loyal group of customers who regarded both him and his company with the utmost respect.

A crack in this relationship opened up one day as Whit visited a regular customer. He could sense in the man's manner that something was wrong.

"I'm sorry, Whit," the agent apologized, "but our account for your product has been turned over to the ABC Company which is selling it to us at 11 percent less than your price."

Whit was too experienced a man to switch from the tactics that had stood him so well. He believed fervently in his company and product story, and determined to stay with it.

He checked with his management which declared flatly that it could not afford to sell for a penny less and still come out with a profit. The company netted three percent on the product

Keep Plugging

Whit continued to call on the lost customer from time to time, citing facts and figures to support his case.

One day, almost two years after the lost account incident, Whit called on the purchasing agent, who welcomed him like a long lost son.

"I'm ready to eat crow," the agent confessed.

He then revealed that his dealings with Whit's competitor had ended disastrously. The company, a major food packer, had shipped out $400,000 worth of canned goods to a large chain for a holiday sale. Because of poor engineering specifications, 35 percent of the cartons split open in transit. To make matters worse, the railroad, fearing further insurance losses, left the entire shipment in various warehouses.

Everybody got hurt. The chain lost a $2 million volume. The buyer nearly lost his job and the vice president responsible for the purchase was fired.

The supplier, of course, was hit even harder. It lost not only the order, but suffered tremendously in prestige and reputation.

Whit did not have to mention to the purchasing agent that his company's cartons were pre-tested to prevent just such an occurrence. The man had heard it several times from the salesman, but had been more interested in bargains.

The upshot was that Whit's firm dispatched trucks to a dozen different warehouses and repacked the goods for the company.

Whit never again had to worry about losing that particular account.

Moral: A price squeeze usually hurts the low price competitor more than the high-quality firm that charges a fair price.

36

Dodging the New Prospect

SEVERAL YEARS AGO A SALESMAN I KNEW TOLD ME OF HIS recurring nightmare.

"It's awful," said Frank. "It starts out with my boss and I standing in front of the Empire State Building. Then he orders me to cold canvass every office in the building. I wake up in a cold sweat."

I studied him for a moment.

"Frank," I said, "I don't want to sound like a psychoanalyst, but will you tell me if you are afraid of cold canvassing in your waking hours?"

My friend didn't hesitate a second. "You bet I'm scared," he admitted. "It takes more guts than I have to be nonchalant about walking cold into an office."

I think I may have helped Frank with some advice I gave him. At least he stopped having nightmares about cold canvassing.

Fear of the Unknown

The advice was simple: Don't be afraid of the prospect. Even

201

if he says "no" it is not a catastrophe. There are plenty of others to see.

Most salesmen shy away from the cold call because of fear of the unknown. We like to call on friendly customers with whom we're on a first name basis. A cold prospect is a stranger and strangers can mean trouble. Such is the way our thinking runs.

In some cases a salesman's fear can mount to the point where he is even afraid of confronting receptionists and secretaries. He is beaten before he actually starts.

After the ice is broken we find that the experience isn't so bad after all. Many salesmen worry needlessly about these calls. I used to fret about them myself until I overcame the fear by simply refusing to be discouraged, despite rebuffs.

Cold-Calling Must Be Organized

Another common weakness in cold canvassing is the disorganized way it's handled. Instead of developing a planned pattern of calls, many salesmen hit prospects in a spotty, time-wasting manner.

One of these men was Ralph Swann, who was assigned a territory in a large midwestern city. Equipped with 30 or 40 accounts, Ralph was making a fair living. Management, however, felt there were another 250 potential customers who should be cultivated in the area. Ralph was urged to get to work on them, but nobody told him how to go about it.

Ralph was selling business forms which could be used in almost any office. His accounts were scattered around the city, which meant that much of his time was consumed in traveling.

To make matters worse, he made a few cold calls on possible leads, most of whom were in still other sections of the territory. This meant more time and mileage stolen away from selling.

Even promising leads seldom panned out because Ralph could not bring any enthusiasm into the calls. He was afraid of the cold call and this chilled any interview. His trials were multiplied when he took on a new prospect after a warm, friendly interview with one of his regular customers. The change was too much for him.

In sales meetings and casual talks with other salesmen, Ralph tried to find the key to making the successful cold call. It wasn't easy. Two or three of them seemed to have mastered the art, but they neglected to explain their secret to Ralph.

The need for expanding his accounts began to be very important to Ralph. He had a growing family and expenses were piling up. He decided that he (1) had to lose the fear of making the cold call, and (2) devise a system for the calls that was simple and economical.

There's a Million of Them

He was pondering the problem with his wife one night when he said suddenly:

"Ralph, you gave up smoking two years ago. How did you do it?"

He was taken back. "Why, I don't know," he replied. "I just quit, I guess."

"Exactly," his wife said. "You just quit."

"But I don't see what that has to do with making the cold call," Ralph said.

Mrs. Swann smiled. "The connection is obvious," she said. "Just walk into an office and ask to see the man in charge."

"Supposing he refuses to see me," Ralph countered. "That's what scares me."

"Then go to another office," his mate responded.

He hugged his wife.

That was it, Ralph decided. Why worry about a turndown at one office when there were dozens to visit.

He worked out a very simple plan. After calling on a regular customer in a particular building, he would systematically cover as many offices as time permitted in the same building. This involved no extra travel and saved him many hours of time. Occasionally, he would canvass a nearby building or two.

The important fact, however, was that the canvassing paid off. Cold calls, he discovered, could become quite hot and profitable. Some of his largest accounts grew out of such prospecting. They remained lifelong customers.

The plan worked so well that Ralph didn't have time to become discouraged or even think very much about the system. If he drew a "no sale" he smiled, thanked the person and was on his way to the next prospect. His territory expanded so rapidly that his firm put two men under him for training. Ralph gets an override on all the business these men develop.

Many of today's most successful salesmen built their territories just by making a door-to-door canvass of every firm that could use their products.

An insurance salesman with a yearly income of $150,000 began his career as a house-to-house brush salesman.

Today, he will approach a complete stranger on a train and sell him a $50,000 policy with ease. He had done it often.

Many companies make it a policy to have their salesmen begin making cold calls right after their training and indoctrination period.

I can tell you one thing: Sales aren't made by dawdling over coffee or taking two-hour lunches. The man who seeks success must use every available minute of the day. Selling time is precious and should not be squandered. There is gold in those cold turkey hills, but it can only be extracted by sufficient exposure.

If a salesman shrinks from exposure he should not be selling. Face-to-face confrontation between buyer and seller is at the heart of salesmanship. Gloomy predictions that the salesman is a vanishing breed are so much nonsense. He is here to stay.

The initiative for the seller-buyer meeting must come from the salesman. If he waits for a written invitation or an ac cidental encounter on the street he and his family can expect a lean year.

The Impact of the Personal Meeting

There are many tools for moving goods. At times the telephone can be used to advantage. Promotion and advertising help. Merchandising and display techniques play important roles. But none of these methods can match the powerful force of person-to-person selling.

Some salesmen avoid cold canvassing by a curious form of rationalization. Their reasoning goes something like this: Only a guy selling potato peelers goes out cold. The really big producers operate differently.

They have "contacts" that smooth the way for them; they don't have to resort to anything as crude as the cold call.

I have news for the salesman who thinks this way. The top producers in this business got that way largely through sheer guts. At rare intervals someone might have eased the way to a particular prospect but most sales were made on initiative. They just walked in, stuck out their hand and started selling.

Index

A

Abbott, Larry, 179
Accounts (*see* Customers)
Activities, outside, value of, 158
Advanced sales training, 79-80
Advertising, 27, 34, 88, 190, 205
  by competition, 190
  "second-generation," 27, 29
Aggressiveness, importance of, 61
Aids, audio-visual, 165-171
Akers, Jim, 150-151
Anderson, Walt, 57-60
Appearance, personal, influence of, 12-13, 18, 58, 97, 173, 183, 184, 197-198
Appraisal, self-, value of, 2, 57-63, 183-188
Approach, glad hand, overdoing of, 174-176
  organized, importance of, 3
Arguments in handling of objections, 102-103
Armstrong, Pete, 147-149
Ashmore, Barney, 65-66
Attrition, customer, law of, 32-37
Audio-visual aids, 165-171
Automation, 23-24, 25-26
Avocation, importance of, 19-21

B

Bad habits, correction of, 183, 184, 186
Baker, Clint, 140
Banning, Keith, 178-180
Benefits, customer, emphasis on, 9-10, 17, 60, 177-182, 191, 197

Big orders, 83-89
  competition for, 86
  follow-up of, 84-89
  incubation period of, 84
Bonwit Teller, 121
Broadening of product line, 126-132
  problems in, 127-129
Bryant, Jack, 103
Burns, Joe, 25-26
Business cycle, effect of, 74
Buyer, bypassing of, 70-76
  friction with, avoidance of, 75-76
Buying committee, 88
Buying decisions, makers of, 48-52
Buying motivations, 74, 179, 181
Buying policy, customer, checking of, 72-73

C

Calls, cold, 201-205
  on customers' customers, 27-31
  dry-run, value of, 43-47
  enjoyment in, providing of, 11-13
  follow-up, 84-89
  missionary-type, 35-36
  perseverance in making of, 14-17, 86-88
  priority system for, 136
  repeat, reasons for, 8-9
    sales presentation in, variety in, 7-13, 84
  refreshments, serving of in, 12
  on retailers, 27-31
  third-party, 27-31
Campbell, Arch, 127-129
Canvassing, cold, 201-205

U

Underhill, Cliff, 137
Unethical tactics, 122-125, 151-152
  price cutting, 130-131, 147-149,
    156, 194-200
Unnaturalness, avoidance of,
  118-119

V

Vacations, benefits of, 158-159
Variety in sales presentation, importance of, 7-13, 84
Volume, low, diversification as
  panacea for, 126-132
  problems in, 127-129
Vulgarity, avoidance of, 118-119

W

Waiting game in sales presentation,
  51
Warm-up presentation, dry-run
  call as form of, 46
Watson, Thomas J., 86-87
Westinghouse Corporation, 128
Widening of product line, 126-132
  problems in, 127-129
Wilson, Frank, 69
Wilson, Jack, 108
Workers, company, obligations of
  to salesmen, 133-134
  salesmen's obligations to, 39-42

Y

"You" element, use of, 160-164